Where to Begin

Where to Begin

A Guide to Teaching Secondary English

Jane Kearns

Boynton/Cook Publishers
Heinemann
Portsmouth, NH

Boynton/Cook Publishers
A division of Reed Elsevier Inc.
361 Hanover Street
Portsmouth, NH 03801–3912
Offices and agents throughout the world

Acquisitions Editor: Carolyn Coman
Production Editor: Renée M. Nicholls
Cover Designer: Jenny Jensen Greenleaf
Manufacturing Coordinator: Louise Richardson

Library of Congress Cataloging-in-Publication Data
Kearns, Jane.
    Where to begin : A guide to teaching secondary English / Jane Kearns.
        p.   cm.
    Includes bibliographical references.
    ISBN 0–86709–406–0 (acid-free paper)
    1. English language—Study and teaching (Secondary)—United States.   2. Language arts (Secondary)—United States.   I. Title.
LB1631.K36   1996
428.0071'2—DC20   96–20719
                                                            CIP

Printed in the United States of America on acid-free paper
99 98 97 DA 1 2 3 4 5 6

For the reason I am a teacher: my students

Contents

Preface: To Teach

I developed callouses trying to make my dreams work, but my dreams never developed callouses.

—W. Eugene Smith, *Images of Man*

I remember well my first teaching assignment—seventh- and eighth-grade English. The day before students came, my principal handed me two grammar books, one for each grade level. "This is what you teach." I was also given lots of advice on how to keep the students under control and in order, how to spot troublemakers, and how to keep the classes busy. I was given *lots* of advice on how to keep them busy, most of it centered on these two grammar books.

And keep them busy I did. We started on page 1: how to answer the telephone for the seventh grade and how to talk on the phone for the more mature eighth graders. We did every exercise, unit, and example, writing out complete sentences, questions, and answers. The busywork kept my four classes in order but left me lost in a trail of ink. The paperwork from my teaching began to take over the room, my car, and my study at home. I couldn't keep up—but the classes were busy and in control. I thought I must be teaching, but I didn't feel like a teacher.

Just before the paper pile toppled down and erased me from the teaching planet, I transferred to a high school. My first day as a high school teacher, the English department head handed me a grammar book and a literature anthology. "This is what you teach." But I knew better by then. I knew not to start at page 1 and chase knowledge all the way through and not to assign every question. I knew I was teaching students, not this book. How I would do this was still a mystery to me but I would keep searching, like Indiana Jones looking for the legend of the lost teaching archive.

The term *writing process* sounds like a package or a predesigned set of formulas: attend a few workshops, pass out folders, assign journals, and we will all be transformed magically into Linda Rief, Nancie

Atwell, or Tom Romano. But why did things work for Nancie and Linda and Tom? Why did they teach that way? Why did each succeed?

I don't know about you, but I have never had a student like those described in most writing process books. My kids are the ones who ask "Does this count?" or "What time does this period end?" One boy told me he had finished his composition and then asked, "So, can I go to the cafeteria for the rest of the year?" These are my students.

When you and I write books describing the development of our students, we might leave out those incidents and focus on our students' success stories too. But other teachers will wonder where we got such super students. To emphasize teaching and learning we highlight the positive. And that's right. But we can't just dream of having perfect classrooms like in the books. An old Irish saying tells us, "You'll never plough a field by turning it over in your mind." We can't dream of perfect classrooms. We have to start with the students in front of us.

In Eudora Welty's gentle little book *One Writer's Beginnings* (1984), she explains she couldn't be a teacher because she didn't have that "instructing turn of mind." I often think of that phrase when I'm preparing a class or a workshop. Having an "instructing turn of mind," I think, is knowing how we learn and how students learn. It's about being teachers and learners at the same time. It's seeing potential, making use of the opportunities and possibilities we see in our rooms, and looking for moments of significant change within students. It's when we first understand something in a new light. Don Murray (1994) calls it response teaching and response learning.

Richard Feynman (1986) mused that "the drawing teacher has the problem of communicating how to draw by osmosis and not by instruction while the physics teacher has the problem of always teaching techniques, rather than the spirit of how to go about solving physical problems." This dilemma of balancing teaching style with learning styles runs through all elements of teaching and is a constant struggle of teachers. Instructing turn of mind is like that: complexities in simple shapes.

FOR FURTHER READING

Feynman, Richard. 1984. *Surely You're Joking, Mr. Feynman: The Adventures of a Curious Character*. New York: Norton.

Murray, Donald. 1984. *A Writer Teaches Writing*. 2d ed. Boston: Houghton Mifflin.

Smith, W. Eugene. 1973. "Between Birth and Death: An Affirmation of Life." In *Images of Man: Concerned Photographers Program.* New York: Scholastic.

Welty, Eudora. 1984. *One Writer's Beginnings.* Cambridge: Harvard University Press.

Acknowledgments

This book evolved from learning and teaching moments with thousands of students, educators, family, and friends. I cherish and applaud them all but with special thanks to the following:

Don Murray, who said I *should* write a book, and Tom Newkirk, who told me I *would.* Both rescued my teaching life: Don with his enthusiasm for teaching and writing and his advice on how to write a book, and Tom with his friendship, humor, and unwavering belief in me.

The people at Heinemann, especially Renée Nicholls and Carolyn Coman.

The wonderful teachers I learned from, especially Theres Gaillardetz, Vianney Fulham, and Antonio Johnson, RSM.

All the students who joined me in this adventure, including those of Gossler Park School, and Memorial and Central High Schools.

Those teachers in Manchester, New Hampshire, who enter their classroom everyday with spirit and spunk. What a joy it is to learn with you and from you. There are too many to list; you know who you are.

The principals and staff of the Manchester schools.

Pat Gorman and Chris Nelson. I learn everytime I join in planning, presenting, and evaluating a workshop. Manchester is lucky to have you both.

The teachers and students of the New Hampshire Writing Program. For ten summers I relished your energy: Maureen Barbieri, Terry Moher, Carol Avery, Ellen Blackburn Karleitz, Tom Romano, and especially Jack Wilde and Paula Flemming.

The Manchester Literacy Portfolio team. For six years I was privileged to research in this collaboration of exciting educators. The University of New Hampshire Writing Lab researchers taught me questions are better than answers, especially Julie Brooks, Carol Wilcox, Kathy Staley, Dan-ling Fu, Lisa Lenz, Kathe Simons, Patty Hicks, Pat Aichele, Doug Kaufman, and Andrea Luna.

The Manchester portfolio research team of Jodi, Karen H., Karen B., Barbara, Chris, Brenda, Maureen, Jim, Diane, Nancy, Kathy, and

Jane C. I am especially grateful to Jane Hansen for her quiet, elegant leadership.

Don Graves. A leprechaun for sure! You sprinkle learning sparks every time you speak and write.

Linda Rief, a consummate teacher and writer.

Mary Ellen Giacobbe, who collects white horses for friends.

Judy and Bill Egan. When I visit your Canterbury Children's Center, I want to be a first-grade student again and open that bag of Frost poems, write in my nature observation book, study water pressure in a real brook, and stop everything when a blue heron comes to the pond.

Those who first took a chance on this unknown workshop presenter: Jim Bowman, Karen Steinbrinke, Jean Roach, and Mike Ford.

My background music: Andy Narell, David Benoit, Muddy Waters, B.B. King, Earl Klugh, George Benson, Harry Connick, James Taylor, Eric Clapton, Makem and Clancy, Mary Black, and always Kermit the Frog, because it isn't easy being green.

People live in one another's shadows and I am lucky to live in the shadows of many friends: Jodi, Rick, Crawf, Grail, Irene, Judy and Jim, Marylou and Joey, Linda Carol, Linda Mac, Pat, Ronda, the *J* team (Jean, Jean, and Judy), John and Kathie Ann, Reet, Judy W., Barbara, Cindy, Heidi, Annie B., Kathy, Debbie, Carol Ann, Chris, Bonnie, Conni, Joannie, Dawn, Betts, Myrna, Ann H., Donner, and David.

My extended Kilrain family. Bless you for letting me win the for-entertainment-only Final Four pool every year! What would I do without you? If I could choose a family, I choose you.

My aunt Esther Nahil, who early in my life taught me that teaching was about joy and laughter.

My mother and father, who started this merry-go-round. From my father I learned to wonder and wave; from my mother I learned to love quiet reading moments when you can hear snow falling. What more can parents give?

Colleen Kearns Desmarais! You made all the difference in my life. Without you I would not be. (Thanks Colleen!) To her Paul, Eric and Zachary, to Web and B.J., Nina loves you all very much. Slainte!

Introduction:
On Becoming a Teacher

I don't believe I can really do without teaching.
—Richard Feynman,
Surely You Must Be Joking, Mr. Feynman

Visiting a colleague's classroom not too long ago, a first grader asked me, "Do you want to be a teacher when you grow up?" Elizabeth's question caught me by surprise. She had just shared her reading journal but obviously paid no attention to my graying hair or my bifocals. Elizabeth waited for an answer as I hesitated, still trying to comprehend the graciousness of her question.

"Are you going to be a teacher?" she asked again.

I nodded.

"Me, too," she said. "I think you'll be a good teacher."

In one quick interchange this young student accepted me as another learner in her class and indirectly suggested her teacher as a good model for us both to emulate. Elizabeth reminds us that we are always learning, regardless of age. I hope Elizabeth does become a teacher because she already knows one of the most important concepts of teaching: caring.

I always wanted to be a teacher. Someone told me once not to admit this because it "sounds like you have no ambition." Well, I think it is a grand ambition. What could be more ambitious than working each day with independent beings who have thousands of questions and who challenge us with their curiosity? What could be more ambitious than finding out where each student is waiting intellectually and then guiding these individuals to reach far beyond for heights they never thought attainable?

What could be more ambitious than opening gates to the future, to mold students into original thinkers? What could be more ambitious than keeping up-to-date with ever-illuminating research on teaching and learning and then culling the ineffective strategies? What could be more ambitious than knowing when each idea is best suited for the lesson and, more importantly, the child?

Our ambition is to instruct, explain, observe, demand, nurture, and share so that others may cultivate a healthy love for learning. We want ideas to spring forth from the students. We teach so others may learn to love learning. Isn't this the richest ambition? When you see a teacher, know you are looking at an ambitious person, a catalyst who is working with the most exciting and challenging of forces: young learners.

My mother said she knew I was interested in literacy from my scribbles on our kitchen walls. I only remember reading and writing being a natural part of life in my home: sitting on my mother's lap listening to her read *Wynken, Blynken, and Nod, Charlotte's Web, Ali Baba and the Forty Thieves, Hans Brinker and the Silver Skates,* and Carl Sandburg. And writing was naturally part of my growing up. Mom and Dad wrote; so did we.

I have always been interested in reading and writing and in being a reader and writer. But along the way I was detoured by my high school "creative writing" teacher and her assigned writing. One weekend (we never wrote in school except for a test) she assigned a descriptive paragraph. I wasn't exactly sure what "a descriptive paragraph" was, but that weekend I saw a full fall moon coming out of the ocean's horizon. The moon fell across the water, all peach and coral and tangerine, and a late-returning sailboat washed across the moonlight. My Dad said that was as descriptive a paragraph as he'd ever seen. "I think that's what you should write." It was fun trying to find the words to sketch the scene. When the teacher returned the assignment to everyone, mine had no grade. She just said, "You copied this!"

There were still elements of that teacher present in my own instruction when I started teaching years later. I taught students English: reading, language use, grammar, vocabulary, and spelling. I knew all the important words: "Get out your grammar book," "Everyone turn to page 48," "Underline all the nouns," "Circle, parse, and diagram." And even though my students seldom wrote an idea of their own, I was happy to be teaching writing. Once in a while the teaching was even fun. I'd shut off the lights, pull the curtains, and we'd groove to the Moody Blues or Simon and Garfunkel.

I was dissatisfied with my teaching and my results. And then in 1971 I went to a writing conference. The instructor, a wonderfully gentle man with a shock of white hair and warm, searching eyes, said hello, handed us all small pieces of paper, and said, "Write for ten minutes." Then he started to write.

I went into a trance. "Did he say write? Write?" I couldn't think of my name, never mind something to write about. "He wants me to write? Write? What the heck does he mean? What does he want? Write? On paper—without a specific assignment—without an outline. How long does he want it?"

Before I even got started, he said, "Stop writing. Look over what you have written and select one of those ideas. Then write another ten minutes on that idea." I was looking at a room full of moving pencils and my blank sheet of paper, which I was supposed to develop into another page.

Well, I survived that day and the instructor, Don Murray.

I still have those pieces of paper and—like my father did with the first dollar he ever took in at our summer store—I treasure them as my first real writing since my dubious moon description almost eighteen years before.

I went home, bought Murray's *A Writer Teaches Writing* (1968), and over the next several years honed my teaching of writing. I was lucky: no one pushed writing on me, so I was able to work out a long apprenticeship in the relative quiet of my classroom. In those years, I tried every suggestion and variation of Don's "smorgasbord" of lesson plans. My classes became a testing ground and I loved it. Some techniques worked and some did not, but I was learning about writing and the teaching of writing.

My copy of Murray's first edition is now worn and held together with an elastic band, but it is still valuable, my first resource. He has since written a newer edition (1985) that is entirely different that I also love, but his first edition's words and enthusiasm made a change in me and in my teaching. He invigorated my teaching and gave me back my love for writing.

From experimenting with Murray's suggestions, I learned to plan an inner structure so that the class looks natural and easy. Like Murray, I try to keep students at the center of my planning. And I became more responsive to what the students need rather than what I thought they needed or what textbook editors told me they needed. With Murray as a guide, I put my grammar book on the reference shelf and replaced it with folders full of paper for students to practice their writing.

Another change based on Murray was the class writing anthology. I used to put it together at the end of the year as a culmination of the class's work until I realized students missed the experience of reading each others' papers throughout the whole year. I start the writing anthology during week one and keep it going, adding the best of each unit, and making sure that every student is represented. Of all the books on my writing resource table, this student anthology has been everyone's first reading choice.

From Murray's example, I also learned to take the best from the best teachers around me, no matter what their department. The math teachers, for instance, often start their class with a short lesson, sending several students to the board to work out problems for all to see, and then the teachers spend the rest of the period moving around the room. I tried that in my writing classes with sentence structure and found it worked.

I visited an art class the students raved about to look for what was unique and special. The students knew exactly what to do when they entered the room; materials were easily available, varied, and plentiful. Each student had a tray and place to store work, finished and unfinished. The teacher started the class with a brief review of the project's purpose—no lectures, just guided comments about the current focus. Then he checked with the students. "What will you be doing today? Will you still be working on the same project? How did you solve the problem you had yesterday?"

Everything was positive; there was an undertone of belief that the students would succeed. This large group meeting was followed by action—a hum of involvement, even excitement. The teacher moved around, stopping at some easels to ask questions, listen, look, encourage, remind, coach, or suggest. He encouraged risk taking and always searched for the potential. Having students' artwork on display created an atmosphere of success and community stature. A variety of forms, angles, and visions were invited. It was obvious that a high value was placed on art and artists. These were the elements I wanted in my literature and writing classes, so I adapted many of the art teacher's techniques into my English classes and they worked. My students planned, drafted, reread, proofed, and published. They began to know how to go about writing.

For seven or eight years I evolved as a teacher of writing but I was mostly alone, finding only a few articles on the subject of writing—until I experienced another touchstone in my education. In the summer of 1979, I attended the Exeter Writing Program (EWP) on the campus of Phillips Exeter Academy. These four weeks were a total immersion into writing and teaching and learning. The workshop pulled together Murray's lessons and my own experiences and experiments, then pushed me further as a writer and a teacher. It taught me to share my writing and my experiences in teaching. Here I met Tom Newkirk, who was to play an important role in my life, as well as Paula Flemming, Jack Wilde, Dennis and Chris Robinson, and Fred Wolff. And Murray was a guest writer.

At the same time I was shedding my old skin at the EWP, other events were happening that affected my teaching. Another University of New Hampshire instructor, Don Graves, was spending three years in a classroom in tiny Atkinson, New Hampshire, publishing his observations in *Writing: Teachers and Children at Work* (1983). And I began writing—articles for the local paper on weekend women's tennis tournaments—which were not otherwise covered by the male-dominated sports room. This forced me to write real stories for real reasons with a critical audience: the players and people who were there at the tournament. I loved the challenge of watching a match and waiting for the turning point when one person won and another lost. I still think this kind of assignment is one of the most challenging for any writers.

I include these pieces of varied information to show that becoming a writing teacher is not a neat, straight line. Becoming an effective teacher means to always be on the lookout for new materials, visions, and insights to share with your students. Nothing is too insignificant not to be a piece of your teaching. Everything we do is a piece of becoming a teacher. There is learning to be found under and near the oddest of trees.

Since that summer in 1979 at EWP I have been teaching, learning, and writing with renewed vigor. I started giving workshops on the writing process. By preparing a workshop on what works in my writing classes, I have to synthesize what I do and why I teach that way. Preparing a workshop is a learning activity for me.

Another experience that influenced my teaching arose from meeting an outstanding first-grade teacher. Mary Ellen Giacobbe taught me much about understanding my role as a writing teacher; she is the reason I have a greater awareness of process teaching. We first met in the winter of 1981. Don Graves had selected Atkinson for his research because Mary Ellen, Judy Egan, and some other teachers were dissatisfied with basals, repetitive simple drill sheets, and busywork.

That spring she invited me to visit her first grade class—I hadn't been inside a first-grade class since I was in first grade. But I agreed to go, if only for a few minutes, an hour at the most. I stayed all day, sat with her writers and readers, and saw for the first time the writing process in the clear form of the true beginning writer. Her students knew exactly what to do when they entered the room and where all materials were kept and available to them without asking. I saw whole class meetings where students discussed issues. Her first graders made more independent and responsible choices than my seventeen- and eighteen-year-olds. These munchkins ran a class lending library with the most popular selections being each others' published books.

I asked Mary Ellen where the alphabet was—every grammar school teacher hangs the letters up around the room. "I thought it was a rule," I chided her. "Look around. It's where they need it." I found it neatly at eye level near the writing table, right where it was needed and not looming overhead. And like the alphabet, Mary Ellen was an integral part of the class: a coach, suggesting, searching for potential, encouraging. Her room was a kaleidoscope of learning.

The excitement of her room was like snorkeling in the Caribbean —colors, tones, and shapes all came together to make magic. And the students accepted me as an another reader, a partner in their process. I learned much from Mary Ellen that day, and I am still learning from her today.

Since then I have spent many hours in many different classrooms writing with students and listening to their stories and their writing techniques. Since those early days I have found real teaching strategies, ideas that would help students appreciate their language, want to be lifetime readers, and understand how writing is a process.

There's a wonderful rhythm to a good, effective writing workshop classroom: drafts shuffling; folders being opened and reexamined; papers brushing over papers; resource books opening, being skimmed and then shutting; conferencing in whispers; writers struggling and seeking help; readers scanning drafts, sketches, and finished texts on the bulletin board; and chairs scraping along the floor for conferences. In classes like these, time is not wasted. In these classrooms students know how to go about writing, know how to spend their time, and know what it is to learn.

Unfortunately, these classes come along only so often and are the result of hard work, patience, understanding, good humor, and an unexplored chemistry that bonds student to student and students to teachers. We do not have a class with this ethereal quality every year, maybe not even every five years. A school year seems like a long time but it isn't, especially the way secondary schools schedule their time. Each student may average only forty-seven minutes a day of actual English class time (minus pep rallies, assemblies, field trips, and assorted other disruptions to learning). One hundred and eighty days times forty-seven minutes does not constitute much time for learning.

But each year, starting from the minute students enter class, teachers charge forward in a missionary-like attempt to educate the citizens of tomorrow. If the last day comes and we have still not succeeded, at least we tried. And maybe learning happens. I need to think so. I can name ten classes that evolved into powerful working environments, another twenty or thirty that came close, another twenty to thirty that needed one more semester, a large group that needed another full year, and yet another group of classes that sadly enough needed another teacher.

In my career as a secondary teacher I have taught grades seven through twelve, college courses, and adult writing courses. I am now a writing teacher trainer. Since my first encounter with a "real" writer, I have achieved a better understanding of how authors write and how to use this information to help my students. I am more comfortable with conferences, stay away from the front of the room, try to get students to have empathy for each other's writing, and connect reading and writing. In fact, one of the biggest changes is teaching literature more like I steer my writing class. I now know that the writing process isn't one set of techniques. It isn't a fad, ready to be tossed aside. It is a living thing, a way of thinking about learning and making sense of life. My teaching changed as I came to understand writing as a process. I don't know any teacher who has "mastered" teaching but we improve as we constantly evolve.

In this book I offer you ideas and strategies that worked for me—specific suggestions to help you develop your writing and literature classes. I hope I also show the joy and passion and challenge of teaching. I hope it makes you think; I hope it makes you want to teach.

FOR FURTHER READING

Feynman, Richard. 1984. *Surely You're Joking, Mr. Feynman: Adventures of a Curious Character*. New York: Norton.

Graves, Donald. 1983. *Writing: Teachers and Children at Work*. Portsmouth, NH: Heinemann.

Murray, Donald. 1968. *A Writer Teaches Writing: A Practical Method of Teaching Composition.* Boston: Houghton Mifflin.

———. 1984. *A Writer Teaches Writing.* 2d ed. Boston: Houghton Mifflin.

Rose, Mike. 1989. *Lives on the Boundary: The Struggles and Achievements of America's Underprepared.* New York: Free Press.

Stillman, Peter. 1995. *Writing Your Way.* 2d ed. Portsmouth, NH: Boynton/ Cook.

1

Before Day One

One technique that I found to work very well for me was brainwashing. I always use it when I write. In fact, I'm using it right now.
—Student

Teaching doesn't start the first day of school, nor does it end the last day each year. Teaching is an all-encompassing lifestyle. With so many options and opportunities to incorporate ideas into the classroom, we need to always be searching for teaching moments. We need to feel comfortable, at ease with young students and their reading and writing.

One way to achieve this comfort zone is by mental and physical preparation outside of class, planning an environment suitable for ourselves as well as for our students. I like to read and reread articles and books that make sense of my teaching and that drive me on. It may be classics by teachers, like Atwell's *In the Middle* (1987), Rief's *Seeking Diversity* (1992), *Lasting Impressions* by Harwayne (1992), or less-direct books like Pirsig's *Zen and the Art of Motorcycle Maintenance* or Patterson's *Photography and the Art of Seeing*. You might want to read books that excite learning such as Bailey White's *Mama Makes Up Her Mind* or *Having Our Say* by the spirited Delany sisters. I am always upbeat and ready to go after rereading the classic challenge *Teaching as a Subversive Activity* (Postman and Weingartner 1969). Good reads like this help me understand the larger picture of learning and then agitate my teaching soul.

Before you begin your teaching, review the school or district curriculum and course requirements. Check what texts are available to you. If the school is new to you, ask for back copies of the student publications; the newspaper will be filled with student opinions and perceptions, the literary magazine will offer rich examples of writing, and the yearbook will fill in the history of your new home.

Visit the school's library. Introduce yourself to the media specialists, who will be valued resources. Check to see if they have a list of the most frequently borrowed titles. What are the students in this school reading? Check the fiction shelves, informational books, magazines, and software. See what computer technology will be available to you. Is there a computer writing lab?

You may also want to plan an overview of the year, but skip lines and keep it flexible. Plan an inner structure so the class looks natural and spontaneous, but be ready to revise your writing and literature programs as you get to know student needs. Keep students at the center of your planning. What is it these students already know? What is it they need and want to know? What is it they are expected to know? And how can you determine all this?

Much depends on the district's requirements and what grade level or course you teach. I do like to develop an overview calendar with possible units listed just to get me going. In a general English class, I first tried writing three days out of five, say Thursday, Friday, and Monday or Friday, Monday, Tuesday schedule. I soon felt I was on a freeway and out of control, a runaway vehicle.

Then I switched to blocks of writing time: the first week and a half of school for writing, then about a ten-day block every three or four weeks that alternated with a literature and language block. I settled on this schedule as it allows me and the student writers time to explore new genres and to develop a piece of writing.

During literature and language units, the students write every day in their reading logs. Time is short so I often have to cut a unit. If I find out that students already are quite proficient in letter writing, personal narrative, or reading novels, then I cut that section. I have cut a Dickens unit from two months to two weeks. Remember the truism that we can do whatever we have to do in the amount of time we set aside. It is true in teaching. Use every moment from the first day, even Fridays, cut days, and field trip days. Every moment is a teaching moment, regardless of attitude, attendance, or interruptions.

Intrusions disrupt our school room, but our job is still to teach each moment. We do not know what technique, moment of silence, or look will affect a student. Good teachers involve students in working things out together, with all individuals building on each other's strength. A good class percolates.

One way to be prepared is to be information rich in what young people are talking about today. How are they expressing themselves? What are current interests? If there is a mall or shopping area near your new school, walk around to observe the atmosphere. What is being sold to these students? Follow this up with a tour of other places available to students, such as historical buildings or art galleries within range of your school. Are there any natural environments that could be used in your teaching? Is there another school nearby where students could share reading and writing? Or an elderly home where the young and old could collaborate?

Learn to take advantage of what is near your school. We teach in a thousand different places, none better than what is right outside your school door. After scouting the backdrop for your teaching, begin to create your teaching environment. Using writing folders is not enough. Writing in class everyday is not enough. Organizing peer response groups is not enough. None of these writing program components will be worth the price of an eraser if we do not also work to build a safe learning climate in our classrooms, an environment in which writing and writers are valued, where risk taking is encouraged, and where mistakes are steps along the learning path.

How can we build this type of climate in our classes? First, we have to understand what it is we are not trying to do in a writing workshop class. We are

- not writing to test for school subjects;
- not using writing for punishment;
- not drilling grammar, spelling, and vocabulary in isolation; and
- not teaching for literary analysis alone.

We also are not trying to produce writing geniuses—the world is already heavy enough with the genius of Shakespeare, Chaucer, Dickinson, Joyce, and Yeats.

What we are trying to do in a writing process classroom is to get students to use language to express themselves, to make meaning through writing. We are packing them with strategies, options, and ideas so they can survive on their own. The physical environment of the classroom should be comfortable, but it does not have to be expensive or architecturally "correct." Teachers and students can quickly transform any room with a few changes and additions: posters, photos of students engaged in writing and reading and conferencing, some drafts bordered by bright construction paper. The physical environment of the classroom should include such things as

- many different kinds of writing paper
- hundreds of pens, pencils, and markers
- notebooks
- dictionaries and word finders
- student papers and work displayed all over
- bookshelves with pleasure, reference, and source books
- telephone directories, filled with every proper name in the area
- magazines, ranging from *Sports Illustrated* to *Skiing* and *National Geographic*
- photo calendars, class photos, and photo books
- a quoteboard
- charts
- folders for source material and writing samples
- collections of the students' best writing
- cartons or boxes to keep student folders
- files for folders of "finished" pieces

And I like to add surprises to keep students observant and to let them know I care about this room too: for a gray spring rainy day, bright yellow daffodils for the writing tables; music playing softly in the background on days filled with publishing routines; new pencils each sharpened into a dagger point for those tough revising days; and hard cinnamon or clove candies on days filled with conferences and final editing.

THE PSYCHOLOGICAL ENVIRONMENT

More important than the physical environment of the room, though, is the psychological environment set by the teacher, which must be conducive to writing, risk taking, and appreciating the other writers in the room. Part of this psychological environment is our belief that students can write and learn. Then we must convince these students that we really like to read their writing and that we want to help student writers. Remember, some of these students have suffered unproductive years—even failure—in English classes. After years of red pens and embarrassment, it may take a while to break down their barriers of distrust.

We establish a safe environment in a multitude of small ways. Share your joy for writing—let them see your topic list and your folder filled with writing over which you struggle. Model the writing process. Be the first reader and writer in your class. Make their assignments your assignments. Remember that the psychological environment includes the whole tone of the room. Here are some rules I set for myself:

- Use a caring and helping voice, never above a conference whisper.
- Encourage writers and readers; don't discourage.
- Help students where they are now.
- Place a high value on reading and readers and on writing and writers.
- Develop an environment for writing, what Murray calls a "climate of thought."
- Develop confidence, responsibility, and respect.
- Offer quiet(ish) time to concentrate, but appreciate the hum of activity.
- Provide time in class for writing and help the writers as they are writing.

Find out what the students like or what interests they have: the school's soccer teams, surfing, music, whatever. Then in newspapers and magazines, find examples of good writing in those areas. Read these articles aloud and post them. Show students that we respect the written word. Fill the room with well-written phrases, sentences, and articles. Ask students to bring in words that surprise them. Challenge them to hear a word today that is new and interesting to them.

Share your joy of reading—let them see you read. Some teachers opt now to provide reading time each day or at least once a week followed by entries written in the students' response log. Model reading during this time and write reactions in your reading logs.

Remove obstacles to writing: workbooks, overgrading, too much analysis of writing models, restrictive busywork such as copying foolish exercise sentences from an English handbook.

Encourage and challenge readers. Find out what they have already read, including what types of books, newspapers, or magazines they continue to read or have at home. Use this information to provide reading in the class but also record this information later so you can challenge them to read in new fields. Record what they *can* do, as Don Graves (1983) suggests. Record growth, not errors.

THE WRITING ROOM

What is it you want students to see and know about you even before class starts? On my classroom bulletin boards and walls, photography is my signature, with large photo posters that are colorful, attractive, and action packed: posters of hot-dog skiers, a middleweight with a lethal left hook, or a tennis player with a dynamite down-the-line backhand. These posters give students a place to rest their eyes and their thoughts; they provide me with large examples to use with the whole class. I also use smaller photos for topic displays and, later in the year, photos of and by students. Once I build up a wide collection, I change these displays about every two weeks. (I knew students noticed when I'd let the current display go for three or four weeks and they would begin to tease me with "Hey, these pictures have been up too long. You running out?")

When you walk into a writing classroom, you should also see students' writing displayed on the wall. Besides a published wall (I call it a "publish and cherish" wall), provide room to display drafts, charts, and drawings. Writing goes up the first week, partly as a sign that this is what happens in this room.

Like a gardener we have to nurture to see growth. A sterile classroom with tiny writing desk arms and hard seats is not my first choice as a place to read or write. But as teachers it is our responsibility to provide students with the most comfortable place possible. Some of the best writing done by my students was in a long and narrow former supply room. The twenty-eight one-piece desks had work areas about the size of a legal pad. But I tried to take advantage of a long wall of windows, a countertop that extended the length of the opposite wall, glorious green glazed wallpaper that made a great background for student papers, a porcelain board students loved to write on, a large open area outside the room perfect for conferences, and a positive attitude. I tried to transfer this attitude to students by talking to them about the need to respect each other's space, work, and time to work alone. Several years and one school later, I was assigned a large classroom and it took me a while to see it as a good learning environment; I had truly convinced myself that cramped was better. In this new room I had bookshelves, bulletin boards and chalkboards, two-piece desks, and huge open spaces. I did not know what to do with all the emptiness.

I've since learned to look at each room like an interior designer—how can I best use the space? The huge corkboards in this new room served as a walking wall. Students, no more than two at a time, could take a break from their work to walk along and read the wall filled with students' writing in process, finished products, my own writing, samples of good writing that students found, my action photos and posters, and often comic strips about writing.

Along the window side of the room, I placed extra chairs for conferences, tables for do-not-disturb-me writing time, and desks to store resources: atlases and almanacs, books of world records, and telephone directories. The conferences were to be whisper quiet, and every other place was designated a no-talk area.

Some secondary teachers provide even more comfort with computers and reading areas. Constance Scully, a junior-high teacher, creates a reading area in her room with a rug, and bookshelves filled to overflowing. She tops it off with pillows and an inviting reading chair. (She learned these techniques from her granddaughter, the product of many whole language elementary classes, who told Conni, "You really have to have easy chairs and a rug.")

I know that many schools today are overcrowded and understaffed so that lots of teachers share rooms. Worse yet is the scenario where you float, teaching in five or six different rooms every day. In these conditions, we carry the appropriate environment with us in our hearts and souls and in oversized canvas bags. Talk to the teachers whose rooms you share to try and use a secure closet or shelf for writing folders. You too will soon convince yourself that moving around every period of the day is the best environment for learning. After all, the students do it all four years.

The best room I was assigned as a writing teacher was in the science wing. The room had sixteen huge, heavy, black immovable biology dissecting tables, along with counters, wooden tables, display shelves, sinks, and even potted plants. As writers, we spread out all over the room with plenty of space to draft, cut-and-paste, conference, proof, and display our published pieces. Extraneous items added to our sensory awareness: unidentified things floating in swamp water, trays of wax with pinned specimens and the odor of formaldehyde that curled the lead in our pencils.

CLASSROOM MANAGEMENT

Research by Graves, Hansen, Elbow, Murray, and Newkirk shows that students learn to write better in a workshop environment. Thus, once we begin to construct a safe environment for writing, the management of our process classroom takes center stage. Throw out the idea of the lecture room in which students sit passively and listen or appear to listen; toss out any vision of a teacher behind the gray desk transferring cultural heritage from college notes. More than the traditional English class, process classrooms resemble art rooms, studios in which not every sketch is graded, teacher direction is short and sharp, and teachers help students when they are in the process of creating. Other requirements include:

- Having a set routine so students know what to do when they enter the room.
- Establishing rules for getting and returning writing folders and for moving about the room to use supplies and the writing center. Routines and rules reduce commotion and make the room more productive. They take out the guesswork, and each minute is precious.
- Talking to students about the use of time, especially if that is an evaluation factor. I tell my students that every minute in class is important so be ready to work precisely as the bell rings. Some schools have a tradition of tolerating late-arriving students and students and teachers who are slow in getting down to business. If the work we do is not important to us, then that message is very clear to our students. In fact, if you are an itinerant teacher, talk to the students who get to class before you. Tell them how you want them to use their time before you arrive. The best writing class is one in which the students get to work on their own whether or not we are there. This is a class we strive to achieve.

TEACHING WRITING

Good writing is not the result of a magic wand; it comes from hard work. Teaching writing is hard work too. People who believe writing arrives magically on the page aren't writers. Writers know that

- Writing seldom comes the first try: good writing is the result of working and reworking.

- Writing doesn't necessarily get easier with time, age, or experience.
- There is no one standard of good writing.
- Correct grammar is not the key to good writing. All writers need to be grammarians, but not all grammarians are writers. As teachers we need to understand and manipulate the balance.

These myths about writing have been attacked by the work of many authors and teachers and books in which writers share their writing process. You will not find in these dialogues an exact writing road to follow, but some techniques may prove useful. In our classes we need to offer students a variety of strategies for writing. When they are on their own, we want them to have at their pencil tips a deep well of options, sources, and ideas.

The climate of the classroom should be relaxed yet productive, with students free to take chances and fail, and develop the discipline needed to be a wordsmith. Since no single approach will get the best out of each student, we need to be like Ulysses, "constantly searching with a hungry heart."

Neither learning nor teaching is neat and predictable, but as teachers of writing we need to see both the larger picture and the details knowing that sustained work will eventually lead toward better writing. It is a weakness of teaching to believe that in nine months we can teach the student everything we know about Thoreau or adverbial phrases or expository compositions. We don't teach what we know but rather what our knowledge, experience, and intuition suggest they need. We understand that each small step in students' learning is just one of many along a long, complex, and capricious path.

How can we develop this teaching tone? Start with what you already know: how to read and ask real questions, how to encourage others to make decisions, how to help people to speak out, how to get someone to listen, how to change the tone of your voice and manner of your talk to suit your purpose and meaning, and how to arrange space in a small room. Build your writing program on these strengths.

As you begin to feel comfortable with writing, your students will feel comfortable in writing class. As you believe in yourself, so must you believe in your students. Educator Herbert Kohl (1989) wrote that all teachers are in different stages of complete renovation. A teacher has to be a construction expert, someone who knows how to draw together skills and resources to create a whole. "Learn how to allow learning," says Murray (1985).

FOR FURTHER READING

Atwell, Nancie. 1987. *In the Middle: Writing, Reading, and Learning with Adolescents*. Portsmouth, NH: Boynton/Cook.

Delany, Sarah and A. Elizabeth Delany, with Amy Hill Heath. 1994. *Having Our Say: The Delany Sisters' First One Hundred Years*. Bellevue, WA: Hall.

Elbow, Peter. 1973. *Writing Without Teachers*. New York: Oxford University Press.

———. 1981. *Writing with Power: Techniques for Mastering the Writing Process*. New York: Oxford University Press.

Fletcher, Ralph. 1993. *What a Writer Needs*. Portsmouth, NH: Heinemann.

Graves, Donald. 1983. *Writing: Teachers and Children at Work*. Portsmouth, NH: Heinemann.

———. 1990. *Discover Your Own Literacy*. Portsmouth, NH: Heinemann.

———. 1991. *Build a Literate Classroom*. Portsmouth, NH: Heinemann.

Hansen, Jane. 1987. *When Writers Read*. Portsmouth, NH: Heinemann.

Harwayne, Shelley. 1992. *Lasting Impressions: Weaving Literature into the Writing Workshop*. Portsmouth, NH: Heinemann.

Macrorie, Ken. 1985. *Telling Writing*. Portsmouth, NH: Boynton/Cook.

Murray, Donald. 1968. *A Writer Teaches Writing: A Practical Method of Teaching Composition*. Boston: Houghton Mifflin.

———. 1984. *A Writer Teaches Writing*. 2d ed. Boston: Houghton Mifflin.

Newkirk, Thomas. 1989. "The Writing Process: Visions and Revisions." Introduction in *To Compose*, edited by Thomas Newkirk. Portsmouth, NH: Heinemann.

———. 1994. *Workshop Five: The Writing Process Revisited*. Portsmouth, NH: Heinemann.

Patterson, Freeman. 1979. *Photography and the Art of Seeing*. Toronto: Van Nostrand Reinhold.

Pirsig, Robert. 1979. *Zen and the Art of Motorcycle Maintenence*. New York: Morrow.

Postman, Neil, and Charles Weingartner. 1987. *Teaching as a Subversive Activity*. New York: Dell.

Rief, Linda. 1992. *Seeking Diversity: Language Arts with Adolescents*. Portsmouth, NH: Heinemann.

Romano, Tom. 1987. *Clearing the Way: Working with Teenage Writers*. Portsmouth, NH: Heinemann.

Shaughnessy, Mina. 1977. *Errors and Expectations: A Guide for the Teacher of Basic Writing*. New York: Oxford University Press.

White, Bailey. 1993. *Mama Makes Up Her Mind*. New York: Vintage.

2

Day One

Reflective teachers . . . are always stepping back to ask, What's work-ing that I can build on? What's not working that I can eliminate?
—Shelley Harwayne, *Lasting Impressions*

Sleepless nights are common for teachers before the first day, fol-lowed by a morning of bathroom stops and a nervous stomach that could propel a nuclear plant. Students are the same. It's the unknown. It wrecks our equilibrium and takes over our imagination. Who will be in class? How will they work together? Will I be able to get them to learn for me and with me?

In early September or late August, students come to school ready to learn. They want a person who is not too mean or friendly, but someone who will respect them as individuals. So if you are cute, clever, or chummy, keep this to yourself that first day! Students aren't ready for cute, clever, or chummy just yet. Try to make day one level, unremarkable, and balanced. Don't show them a syllabus filled with enough work to take you through the next century. And don't pull the I-want-to-be-your-friend routine. Regardless of how close in age you may be to these students, they are not looking for a friend. They want a teacher.

Since I am nervous and they are nervous, I try to ease both our anxieties by being quiet. I usually don't talk much on day one—my nerves crackle my voice, and the students are too busy checking out who else is in the room to listen.

In a calm voice, I point to my name on the board. "Good morn-ing. This is English 1, room 888, period C. Check your schedules to make sure you are in the right room. If you are, please leave your schedules on the outside of your desk so I can sign them. While I'm doing that, fill out this form for me. Quietly please." The form asks for names, addresses, homerooms, their schedules with teachers and room number, and—if they are new students—their former schools.

Then I go around the room initialing the schedules. As I stop at each desk, I quietly say hello and the student's name, looking each one in the eye. This helps soothe my furrowed emotions and gives the students a semblance of order in a hectic, nerve-wracking day. Later I arrange the students in alphabetical order for quick attendance and so I can learn their names. I start at the back of the last row and put the *A*s there, giving the *WXYZ* people a different view of the world. For older students, who even hate reversed alphabetical order, I ask them to fill in a seating chart by rows, and tell them to please sit in the same seats tomorrow so I can learn their names.

I give them a brief one- or two-sentence introduction to the class, emphasizing the reading and writing we'll be doing. Then I get them writing. Writing is easier the first day, as books are often not yet available from the supply room. I want my students to know we will be doing a lot of writing and I want them to have a pen or pencil ready at all times.

THE FIRST DAY'S WRITING

Since most teachers in secondary school have about five classes, I try to have five different, though similar, ways to get each class started.

I might get one class webbing or branching their names. Who am I?
In another, we might begin an authority list: What are some things you are an authority on, at least in this class?
We might brainstorm things we know something about.
I pass out an interest inventory form for another class to fill out.
I might ask students in one class to identify if they are readers or writers. "Pick one, no hedging, and tell me in writing about yourself as a reader or writer."

You can see that though different, each activity results in similar information: an introduction for me to the student and a beginning to the writing process for the student. I look at the papers to see patterns I can build upon to make them better learners and might refer

to them later if the student hits a wall. Somewhere along the year—
a month or two later—I return the first-day sheets and ask students
to update them and put them in their folders.

As the students work on this activity, I take the seating chart and
try to learn all the names right then and there. I can do it if I try. I
want them to know before the class ends that I plan to treat them as
individuals and knowing their names is step one. I make a point to
refer to several students by name: "Josh, would you open the window?" "Bill, do you need a pen?" "Teresa, please collect those
papers." "Can I answer a question for you, Mark?" This name recog-
nition surprises the students and sets up, I hope, that environment
that I think is so important.

As the time winds down, I give them a homework assignment. Yes,
homework on day one. I do this mainly to let them know that the
study of English or composition or literature goes on outside of the
classroom. These home assignments vary every year and from class to
class. They may include:

- Reading a front-page newspaper article and writing a one-
  sentence summary of that article.
- Listening to a news broadcast and summarizing the lead story.
- Making a list of books you have read over the years in school.
- Asking an adult at home how the family happened to live here.

Once I came up with an absolutely brilliant first-day assignment
(Kearns 1996.) "Go outside on your back porch steps just after dusk
and listen. Write down everything you hear." It was a great assignment, and did it bomb.

When I went out and listened on my back steps (I try to do all the
assignments I give out), all I could hear was the wheezing of cars and
trucks. The next day we all agreed this idea failed. One boy who
lived in a rural community outside Manchester said he did hear
interesting things: water gurgling over the rocks in the stream down
beside the pasture, horses clomping around the barn exercise area,
and northern mockingbirds.

We wanted to know more. (This interchange was an important
beginning to the type of sharing I want to develop.) How did you
know what kind of birds? How many animals do you have? Where in
Deerfield do you live? The exercise for the whole class failed, but it
became a shared experience. Writing is often like this—we do not

know what will reach each student so we keep trying. Even a bad, untested idea can deliver some positive results.

As the students leave my class on day one, I stand by the door and again try to look everyone in the eye and say or guess their names. If there is time, I do a go-round, where I recite each of their names. This closure helps to open our relationship for days that follow.

That night, I read Albert Cullum's (1971) book *The Geranium on the Window Sill Just Died But Teacher You Went Right On* to remind me what our students see and hear and think, to remind me I am teaching students, not the subject. And I read through some quotes about teaching. Then I get to bed early. I do sleep well after day one; in fact, I usually need a nap, and an early night, because the rest of our teaching life follows.

FOR FURTHER READING

Cullum, Albert. 1971. *The Geranium on the Window Sill Just Died But Teacher You Went Right On*. Harlin Quist.

Harwayne, Shelley. 1992. *Lasting Impressions: Weaving Literature into the Writing Workshop*. Portsmouth, NH: Heinemann.

Kearns, Jane. 1996. "Day One Dud." In *Oops: What We Learn When Our Teaching Fails*. Edited by Brenda M. Power and Ruth S. Hubbard. York, Maine: Stenhouse Publishers.

3

After Day One

Never forget that teaching is similar to writing, a craft and an art that cannot be contained by absolutes. There is no one way to teach effectively. You have to change as you learn more about your subject, gain experience, face new students.
—Don Murray, *A Writer Teaches Writing*

After surviving day one, we have the whole rest of our teaching year ahead of us. So now what happens? Recent national reports suggest that students write more in science classes than in English and that writing improves until students get to junior or senior high. Whether true or not, this is a strong indictment of English classes that lack writing instruction and practice. We want students to learn to write as well as write to learn. We must establish writing as an everyday activity.

The most difficult part of writing in the classroom is the beginning of each year. Often students do not know about writing as a process or how to work in a writing workshop, or they have forgotten over the slow summer. At the beginning, none of the students has a writing routine in place. Sometimes even new semesters begin this way.

The initial phase of composing is a valuable time and not as simple and one dimensional as textbooks suggest. Whether we call it prewriting, planning, exploring, getting started, or walking around, this initial jump into writing involves students searching what they already know and what possible angles of discovery they can make. And what we often forget is that this prewriting *is* writing.

Writing evolves from general points of departure such as memories, past or current, observations, interviews, readings, or research. Student writers enter class with material but often need help to open up and remember details or to see a sharp focus point. Sources other than memories need time, which is why writing teachers like to start with personal narratives. Memories are available to every student and in totally individual ways.

GETTING STARTED WITH QUICK WRITING

Tapping our memories for experiences that unfold into interesting writing can be accomplished by teaching students a variety of ways to recall and search: mapping, free writing, brainstorming, listing, and webbing. In every case we are trying to get the students to focus quickly on their own topic and write down as many remembrances as they can. These prewritings are not paragraphs but lists, collections of words, phrases, and/or ingredients. Once you stop after three, five, or ten minutes, look back over your words. Check your paper for discoveries, surprises, and connections. Circle or star them. Do they offer a start to your paper or give you a direction to search?

At first prewriting will be difficult but, with practice, it loosens minds and allows free associations. The real piece may be found in the associations, not in the initial thought. This activity may work for some students, but no one approach to quick writing works for everyone. Our job is to introduce the strategies and then give students the option of using ones that work for them. Outlines could be included here; once considered the *only* way to begin, they are too restrictive for me and many developing learners.

In photography we talk about "walking around" the subject, looking for a variety of angles and the best light and depth of field. In writing, brainstorming opens the writing doors of possibilities. Put blinders on, I tell students; don't be distracted by the rest of the world. Tune your head into your selected topic and let your mind take over. Write as fast as you can, don't judge or be selective, just write whatever the mind suggests. Turn ideas around in your head and on paper. Ignore everything in the room; in fact, leave the room with your mind.

As these developing writers collect topics, they may need other techniques to develop more information or details such as interviewing someone else who was at an event. I encourage the use of family photos. If a student is going to write about the pet or the trip to the beach or Uncle Charlie who lives up north, then bringing in a photo opens up a flood of details and allows the student to catapult into a whole new set of ideas. Other activities are question-and-answer lists, charts showing what is already known and what needs to be found out, quick-focused writes, drawing scenes or maps, and answering who, what, when, where, why, and how questions.

PRIMING THE WRITING PUMP

Some teachers like to get a writing sample from every student on the first or second day, but I prefer a more deliberate approach. A full class period of writing early in a course scares students who don't know how to use writing time yet. Others students want constant reinforcement that they are doing the right thing. A variety of small activities in those early classes may assist students with developing a more independent nature as well as a wider scope of things to write about. These are topic search strategies I think students should experience as they build a repertoire about how to go about writing.

I call this priming the pump—putting words on paper before we get writing, exercises that stretch a writing mind and strain the brain. They are tools to get writers thinking and visualizing before composing.

DAY TWO

For me, day two is as important as day one for establishing the psychological climate of the class. I want students to believe early in this class that they and their writing will be received honestly. If they work, they will succeed.

I try to run a similar routine each of these early days, so students early become familiar with how the class works. I want them to understand how they spend their time in this writing and literature class and how to explore ideas and examine, develop, and collect details, a foundation they need to write on their own on any subject and format.

Writers should not lock themselves into a tight, unforgiving outline that is without a glimmer of freedom and spontaneity. No, writers need to walk around their subject. Like an artist, a writer's initial burst should be like a sketch of thin lines and broad impressions, colors, shapes, and textures of possibilities that propel our words into longer pieces of interesting reading.

I launch day two with an activity that calms most nerves and gets them exploring the possibilities of topics. I try for something different in each class, yet similar and related to what we did the day before. I may use a timeline, a bull's-eye target, an authority list, a quick write, or various other short actions that help overcome the blankness of the first page. These exercises help open writing minds and may lead to topics and viewpoints that can later be developed. They are working toward a subject for a short piece of writing.

After I model the quick writing device on the board or overhead, students work on their own as I move about the class. This makes them aware that the teacher will not be at the front of the room. Judging from their body language, we stop (usually after twenty minutes or so) and I may do a quick workshop on the writing center. I want them to move freely to the writing center for supplies.

Then I talk about searching for writing topics. What possibilities came out of the quick writes? Perhaps an incident that only lasted a minute or second but that stayed with them. Perhaps it was a humorous story about a pet or place or person, a childhood incident that is funnier now than then. These initial activities are different ways to tap our memories without having to wait on writing to observe, read, research, or interview.

Writing Folders

I cannot work or teach without folders, and I do not think students can learn to write or develop their writing without folders. Writers collect and look back over what they have done; this seemingly simple exercise is an important prewriting strategy. Writing is hard enough; we don't need to spend wasted time looking for our work. So we need folders.

For younger students I usually write their name on the tab in my version of calligraphy. The folders in my class are texts, more valuable than any grammar book. Within these covers are the students' writing life. I can see their growth, note areas of concern and success, record their writing history, and suggest their writing futures.

Students compile a list of possible topics through an interest inventory, signature analysis, questions survey, and/or authority list. Make sure they know these topics are possibilities; some students fear they will have to write about every single topic listed. Making a list and looking at topic-generating sheets is important because you want students to think about writing from day one, every day, even when they are in another unit. After long weekends or holidays or vacations, I get the folder list going again and have them add a few more ideas. In conversations in class or before or after class, I often ask students if this is a topic they could write about. If so, I suggest they add it to their topic list now and place it in their folder.

I set a few rules about folders. One is that writing folders stay in class. They never go out because this can lead directly to being lost, stolen, or kidnapped by the teenage mutant folder turtles. Individual pieces can be taken out and worked on in other rooms but never the entire folder as they simply disappear.

Also, no one looks at another student's folder. These are personal and not for public viewing; we will not invade another's private writing area. I tell students to not even get a folder for another person unless requested. The only folders you can see are yours and mine, which will always be in some obvious spot in the class.

If needed, I talk to students about writing as a process and what that means to them and the management and contents of their writing folders. Most writing, before it is finished I tell them, goes through a variety of steps such as preparing, composing, polishing, sharing, and proofreading. Notice I left out publishing as not all papers are published in this scheme; it is a decision made later by the student, who can select the best paper to edit, reread, and publish in some manner. Publishing also refers to submitting a paper and its process sheets for grades.

Student writers are learning to use their language and communicate their experiences. In this light, writing process becomes an instrument for growing, thinking, organizing, reflecting, connecting, and speculating. Like an art studio with many things going on, many sketches are created but not every sketch is finished, publicly viewed, or graded. Our writing room is filled with varied activities, and the hum of activity is better than the drone of passivity.

As the students build their collection of drafts, possible drafts, and writing ideas, we also add other pieces of information to the folders. Students keep a list of skills they can do in their folders. Then they check these as they finish a paper and add skills as they practice them in their papers. This is why the folders are important; it is the student's history as a writer and learner!

Writing requires preparation, concentration, study, time, and help. One goal of my class writing is to get them to rehearse writing off stage, to think and carry the piece home with them at least in their heads. Even on day two.

I also want students to start hearing and speaking about writing with a special language: "conference," "draft," "comp" for "composition," and "graph" for "paragraph." Writing is thinking and making connections. Writing helps us reflect, speculate and grow. Their assignment day two is to make a list of a six or seven possible writing topics.

DAY THREE

I remind students on the third day of class that we are all looking for topics to write about. I tell them there is no sure method, but one way to start is by writing a list of possible subjects inside their folders—the six or so from last night plus any they think of today. During this time, I write my list on a transparency with the overhead light turned off. After five minutes or so, I show them what I'm working on and how I go about picking a topic.

My six or seven possible subjects are all within the range of students' experiences. On the overhead I might list baseball blahs, someone I know that I could describe, a pet, and some problem or local issue such as students wearing hats in class. These subjects change from class to class. Some subjects I plan to list, but many are spur of the moment as I overhear conversations between classes.

An overhead is effective because it allows me to face these new classes and search for body language that suggests questions, understanding, and concerns. Also, I can use the transparency for review tomorrow. I let them hear me think aloud about these possible topics and eliminate all but one topic that seems hot today. "Well, I don't have a story for my dog right now that is clear in my head. I'll have to do more brainstorming. Maybe a separate list just about the dog. And describing my niece would be too long. I really like baseball strikes. I hope they never play the game. Move it to Japan or the Dominican Republic but leave us alone. Baseball is boring. It's embarrassing that our national sport is so devoid of action, where a perfect game is when nothing at all happens . . ."

If things go well as I talk, then I'll ask a student to take notes on what I say. Teaching them the importance of taking notes and starting with some words on paper before they write are other activities that work. Students pair up and talk about their possible topic with the listener taking notes for the talker. Each student then starts with some words that may help focus writing.

I star baseball blahs on my overhead. Now it is their turn, and I ask them to take their list of subjects and narrow and eliminate in a similar way. Then I direct them to play an association name game. As fast as they can, I have them write every word, idea, name, and thought that could be related to the subject they are thinking about. They are to put blinders on and keep all distractions out to dig deeply into that topic.

This quick writing is like limbering up before the race. I do the same but not on the overhead. So I sit at a student desk and give it a go. After at least five minutes, I stop and introduce sharing to the class. I tell them we share orally so any deep dark secrets or private things should be kept for home journals. Topics should be something they are willing to share, beginning today with a possible topic. I ask them to listen to the other students to get ideas and write down any possible topics for future papers.

I go around the room accepting each topic with a nod and a thank you. I say their names (so they can learn each others') and I accept everything—super, average, or suspect. The topic isn't the goal here, just the acceptance. I want them to feel that every idea is acceptable and will be received for its possibilities. I also want students listening with the potential of learning orally from one another.

With students who can handle my humor, I may mention my three no-no topics:

Cats. I'm allergic to them mentally and physically and no one ever gets beyond the word *cuddly* in writing about cats.
Disney trips. If we haven't gone yet, we don't want to hear about your good time. If we went, we had a better time.
Parties. I'm too old for teenage weekends.

I change these no-nos as warranted but I keep them honest. But actually I am challenging students to think how they can be specific in their papers. Family trips, pets, and parties are often predictable and dull; I want unique and lively.

If a student is unsure about a topic as we go around the room, I say OK, I'll come back to you later, which I do. I'll push, but not to embarrass. I want everyone's voice heard at least once by the end of day three.

I finally announce homework to brainstorm their memories for details, colors, shapes, action, and sounds and who, what, when, where, why, and how. With luck, when we come in on the next school day (preferably giving them a weekend to think about the paper topic), everyone will be ready to write. I suggest they talk to others in their family for details, to check photos, to list, to draw, to collect, and to quick draft enough to know you have something to write about and a few roads you could follow. I ask them to pursue whatever will get them ready to write and roll when they come to the next class.

DAY FOUR

When they enter class on day four, I am at a student desk, ready to write or already writing. The folders are in full view on the front desk or table. I may ask a student to monitor the folders and to remind students to get writing.

I try not to *start* class when the bell rings; I want students to get to work as soon as they get there. If things go well, the class is quiet by the time the bell rings, except for the compelling sound of pencils scratching and scraping over paper.

If a few students continue to talk, I give them the look, though one student said I really give them "the eye." I stay in the writing position, lift my head, open my eyes wide, and stare. Usually that's enough. But if they continue and I have to get out of my writing, I take a chair, sit down beside the talkers, and ask, "What's the problem?" Then the responsibility is on them to come up with the reason they are not working. This sincere approach gives everyone the message that writing in this class is serious and the routine includes not waiting for the teacher to start class. I want them working on writing. They don't have the right to disturb other writers. They interrupted my writing and better hope I can find the flow when I return to my paper. (Often I'm not really on a topic as I get nervous at this initial stage of the writing class. I so want the students to blend into this routine that I can't concentrate and end up mumbling on paper but I *look* like I'm writing. Once the class settles, I can do some solid writing.)

What I am "really" doing is modeling writing. Strangely, students have not seen many adults write. They see products and are expected to do process, but many need to see composition happening. I write and stop and look up to think. I doodle a bit. I pause. I write very fast, then pause and reread, and then write another line or two. I lift my head, I lean into the papers, and keep going, pencil scraping. I slow down, pause, doodle. Go back to the top of the page, read forward, write some more, skip four or five lines, and turn to the next page. All of this body language modeling shows things I do when I write, but in the quiet of these early classes I want students to see and hear and feel what is happening outwardly when a person writes. After a certain amount of time, I quietly move to any students whose body language suggests a struggle. How much time to wait is hard to decipher. I judge by the body language of the majority of the class. For regular writing conferences, I take a chair or a stool, but for these early talks I try to speak to many students quickly; I walk, squat down and ask, "Are you stuck? Can I help?"

I continue quietly around the room, stopping at any visible trouble spots, and then I stop the class. I say something like, "You've been writing for thirty minutes. Good work. Stretch your fingers or your head. If you really are on a hot topic, continue on, but you can also be sure it will be there when we come back tomorrow. Writing is hard work," I tell them, "but it is fun and challenging and worth the good fight." I congratulate them on their work habits to reinforce more active participation by these students.

DAY FIVE AND THE FIRST WRITING UNIT

Students come in and start writing. Some teachers like to start the writing class with minilessons but I prefer to get the writing going and make sure that I give them the time to write first. I want to establish a writing rather than a listening-to-teacher routine. I then end the class with a clinic.

After ten to fifteen minutes of my own writing, I move about the class searching out students I know were stuck yesterday or who seem to display the language of the writing block.

I conduct conferences on searching for topics or getting started at other times during the day as well, such as when I see students walking the corridor to lunch, in homeroom, in study halls, and even out of school. I use their names and ask what they're writing about and how the writing is going.

By this time I have spoken to every individual eye to eye. I want to build expectations and support while eliminating teacher-to-student barriers, fear of writing class, and most discipline problems. As the students write more, I write less in class and conference more. There is nothing magical about this conferencing. I move around the room, tapping students and cajoling, agreeing, supporting, questioning, and answering them.

Sometime in these early days I begin my clinics or minilessons. Exactly when is hard to say; I watch and anticipate. A clinic on titles is one that most writers need, so my first clinic may introduce this topic. I tell them that titles are not topics and that a title should reveal more after the piece is written than before. Students love looking for titles in words they have already written. "Look at your last two or three paragraphs and see if there is a title already there."

Listing several tentative titles gives us focus. As writers search for a title, we explore the focus of our piece. I will often list some of my sample titles on the board or the overhead. Then I have the students list fifteen titles, way beyond what you normally think of as a lists of titles. (This Murray suggestion works for me personally as a writer and professionally as a teacher of writers.) I direct them to put their topic on the page and list possible titles.

We do a go-round with each student reading one possible title. Students read or say their titles; I accept each one with a thank you but no comments; all are titles by students who are working to be better writers. In a later unit I would probably do the same routine after a clinic on leads. I find these go-rounds break the ice and make students comfortable with their own writing voice for later sharing and group conferences.

These quick and focused end-of-class clinics give me a chance to explain class routines. I have a new bulletin board, I'll say, as I walk to the sideboard. Observation is a big part of writing. Telling details, that's what writers search for and readers want. Colors, shapes, textures, that special glance, an unusual combination that reveals so much in our writing. Short story writer Sean O'Faolain (1978) said he likes "punch and poetry." Poetry is the language that seems just right and punch is the special impact the words have on us.

"The photos on this bulletin board are the results of sharp observations by the people who took them; these are for you to view, a time to relax your writing brains and activate your seeing brain." I point out one large poster and talk about where the photographer was situated, what happened next, and what stands out. What is the person in the photograph thinking or saying, and what details make it an interesting picture?

"Come up and see what artists do with a camera and light; this is what you do with a pencil and words. Maybe one photo will give you a topic idea. Come, but only two or three people at a time. Try writing something like one of these photos; action scenes, for instance, are hard to write, especially present-tense action. Don't disturb another writer on your way up from or back to your seat. No hitting, shoving, pushing, pulling, tugging. And no talking above a church whisper."

I change these photo displays every two weeks, using themes that include faces, places, colors, sports, headlines, news, student photos, animals, space, New Hampshire, or my own photos. Though I will display soccer in the fall and people when we explore character sketches in literature, I'll break the mood with surfing pictures right after a snow blizzard, when cold surrounds every inch of our writing world.

If students have trouble with telling about action rather than showing it through their writing, I display a variety of high-action pictures such as sport photos and pictures in a "decisive moment," as Henri Cartier-Bresson (1952) called it. If the class needs practice in detailing scenes, we select a photo and try to find words that capture its essence. I leave the used photos in envelopes for students to go back to later. Some students will ask me if I have any photos on snowboarding, for instance, which becomes an opportunity for them to start collecting or for us all to search for this sport.

Another opportunity to teach occurs when students ask about my collection of pictures. I tell the students about my joy in searching for new magazines, especially those with great photos. I don't ski but I love *Powder* magazine. I'm really trying to develop inquisitive, observant students who want to learn their whole lives.

During the first writing unit, my clinics are at the end of class. My time is brief and I find that if I begin with a minilesson it becomes a maxilesson and the whole period goes by. To develop a routine of writing in my class, I only use the last five to ten minutes for clinics.

Typically, these clinics begin with little more than housekeeping ideas: how to access the dictionaries, when to use the writing tables, what happens if you forget to bring a pencil, how to use folders, and how to submit papers.

This first writing unit lasts six or seven days. When I tried getting writing samples earlier and in a shorter time, the pieces were usually artificial and slowed down my workshop class. I want a more complete view of the students as workers and writers. My writing sample is as much a learning device for me as it is for them. Much of their school writing up to now has been fast, drafted in one class period and then finished at home. So I slow down.

I want students to learn to write in class in an unhurried atmosphere, and when I set deadlines, I make them flexible: "Wednesday is the last class day you'll have for this paper but you can pass it in anytime between now and the 'deadline'! Friday, at 2:34 PM!"

This soft deadline works for students who need more time and it gives me a range of days—a weekend, perhaps—to read the papers and get them back by the next Monday. I work hard for this quick turnover because all writers like immediate feedback.

Though usually handed in at different times, I hand all these first papers back together. That day I would continue the new unit we were on, say literature, and leave the last fifteen minutes to respond to papers; this clinic is not an ending but a beginning to the next writing unit and to more class management. Positive reinforcement is better than negative. I don't mark up the papers but use sticky notes to write about what I like, what I think is the potential within the paper, and to ask questions.

After handing back the papers, I give the students a chance to read my notes to them. I move around the room, point out good lines, and congratulate them and pat their backs. I try to speak to each student about his paper. I want the end of the first writing unit to be a positive memory.

While students look over their papers and update their folders, I ask one or two students for permission to publish their paper for the next writing unit in a couple of weeks. I type these up or have students type them or print them out on computers.

Quoteboard

Not every paper is an *A*+, but within any paper may be something special—a word, phrase, or line that surprises. Celebrate these potentials. Take the phrase and copy it onto art paper, perhaps writing the line in calligraphy.

What follows are some sample quoteboard gems tucked away inside otherwise forgettable essays:

Cereal: crackly sound like icicles falling from a roof on a cold winter's morning.
My sister is such a brain; she always gets the last hand on the bat, as they say.
Life is too complicated *not* to have an education.
Discoveries open windows in my mind I never knew were shut.
Friends, memories, good times never die; they just deserve a rainy day by the fireplace to be remembered.

Your mind is a time machine: you can remember the past and imagine the future.

Try to learn more than you need to know.

Doodling is a relaxing way of doing nothing.

If you only feel important when other people think you are—you aren't. You have to feel important even when others don't think you are.

To some, laziness is a religion or a cult.

When people think and dream about their heroes, it makes them feel good inside, and that's another type of love.

I like to post these pieces onto shocking fluorescent cardboard and display them on the chalkboard. I read them and as a group we celebrate and applaud the achievement.

FOR FURTHER READING

Cartier-Bresson, Henri. 1952. *The Decisive Moment.* New York: Simon & Schuster.

Murray, Donald. 1984. *A Writer Teaches Writing.* 2d ed. Boston: Houghton Mifflin.

O'Faolain, Sean. Quoted in *Ten Modern American Short Shories.* 1978. New York: Bantam.

4

Literature Reflections and Connections

English and language arts teachers have come to feel schizoid in their classes, using process-oriented approaches to writing and very traditional approaches to the teaching of literature.
—Judith Langer, *A New Look at Literature Instruction*

Once the classes experience their first writing exercises with me, we delve into literature. For this first literature unit, I want a short book such as *The Pearl* that offers an opportunity to explore ideas while allowing students to read the book quickly. In order to get a sense of what they know, I may have all classes reading the same title. Besides the basic reading and discussion of Steinbeck's story, characters, and style, I also introduce students to the reading log.

READING REFLECTIONS

Mature readers often mark up their books, highlight sections, or make notes inside the back cover. Students using class books or school anthologies cannot do this, so the next best way to be engaged daily with the words on the page is with a log, daybook, or reaction journal. The name isn't important, only how these writing notes are used. I want my students to read with a pen or pencil in their hands to record thoughts and to encourage close observation of the writer's words.

I prefer a balanced approach to writing with literature through a combination of assigned writing and free-choice writing. If you leave it all free choice with students unused to making decisions, the entries often turn into simple summaries or sophomoric confessions, neither of which are the goal of English courses. On the other hand, if the writing is all assigned, students never have the opportunity to explore and reach out on their own trails of thought. I see my role not so much as helping students to understand every aspect, theme, and nuance of this reading as helping students to become lifelong readers and critical, creative thinkers.

Assigned writing helps students know what they can write about and allows them to write in genres or styles or directions they might not otherwise try. Many adult readers are also given specific writing formats that their responses must take. With assigned writing, students participate in the discipline of writing processes.

I try to make my assigned writing challenging and open ended. Since I would not grade each one of these entries on an individual basis, students are encouraged to take risks. I tell students their answers should not be alike and that I want twenty-eight different responses. This diversity doesn't often happen, but my point is I don't want students to be afraid to risk and possibly fall short of other work they do. I want them to try something new, to go out on their thinking limbs.

Questions for the Reading Log

How can we demand written literary analysis when we know the literature itself is often quite distant from students' everyday living? The answer is to connect students' life to the literature we have them read. "What are the implications for you in this story or in these characters? Put yourself in there. Have you ever been or felt alone? How was your experience similar to these characters? How were your feelings and reactions different?" By making students connect the words on the page to the realities of their lives, the literature becomes more of a mirror and less of a mirage. Depending on the text, I might have students consider questions such as:

Did Kino lose everything and gain nothing?
Does this remind you of any experience you've had or heard of?
What would you have done?
Have you ever had a day like this?
Do you know two people who are so different?
Education was freedom to Kino. What freedoms has education given or
 will give you?

What form do your dreams take?

How would you have acted?

What else could the character have done here?

What effect does the author achieve through these words? Why do they work? What did the author do to get them to work?

Why does this happen here?

How does the author move the story along here?

What questions do you have about the way the author pieced the story together?

Why is the first sentence first? How is it related to the ending?

Read a passage that you particularly liked. What struck or surprised you?

Encourage students to take chances by not grading every reading log entry. And any of these assignments can be developed into longer papers. Encourage your students to use these thoughts, reactions, reflections, and connections in their essay exams. We want our students not only to write about the literature but to use the readings as springboards to expression. And we want them to have many options to choose from when they do communicate in writing.

For instance, after reading *The Pearl*, I might ask students to write about risks they have taken or for whom or what they might risk their life. Would they throw back the pearl? Students could take a suggestion, or they always have the choice to go off on their own and write a response to a specific idea generated from the reading. This option of free-choice writing in their logs gives students more practice in thinking about the reading, reacting to the piece, and evolving their own format. The story isn't in the words on the page but in the words that connect the reader with the writing. Our job as English teachers is to bring students to the world created within the literature.

LITERATURE CONNECTIONS

Throughout the rest of the year, reading logs reflect students' reactions and growth as readers and thinkers. Most of the responses will now be free choice, enabling students to demonstrate their thinking. Occasionally I use a shared experience, such as reading several of one author's books. One strong occasion evolved from our exploration of the picture books by Byrd Baylor. I read her *I'm in Charge of Celebrations* (1986) and we discussed Baylor's celebrations, wondered what celebrations she'd have if she lived in New England, and shared our own celebrations orally and then in writing over the next few weeks. I ended the initial Baylor class with a rereading of *Celebrations,* trying to emphasize that good books can and sometimes should be read several times. I wanted students to leave the classroom with Baylor's words echoing in their heads.

The next day I brought in copies of Baylor's other books for students to spend time reading, sharing, writing notes in their logs, and looking at Peter Parnell's drawings. (I had gathered as many of these books as I could get from my own collection, school libraries, the city library, and from friends' bookshelves.)

Over the next few days we watched a video of Baylor reading her own work. We could also have watched one of her books that has been animated or a program featuring Parnell's artwork. We read an article or two about Baylor, checked the author biographies in the library, and read an interview with her. And wherever I could, I added my own knowledge gathered from meeting her, listening to her speak, and getting my books autographed. Indeed, one reason I selected Baylor is that she is a personal favorite and I have firsthand stories to share both about hearing Baylor and Parnell and about my own readings of Baylor's books at workshops for teachers. By doing this I want to take students both far away from the actual words on the page to see where their reading can carry them and also bring them back again to the words on the page.

We might talk about what kind of a person we think Baylor is. What would be important in her life? Where does she stand on conservation issues or on human rights? Which of us in class would like Baylor or Parnell as a dinner companion? These discussions are not meant to uncover the exact answers as much as they are meant to develop an understanding of how printed words on a page give insights to who we are as writers and then as readers, and how we can move beyond reading and blaze our own thinking trails.

All along this journey into the words of Baylor and images of Parnell, students are talking, listening, observing, thinking, reading, and rereading. These activities combine to give students a wider foundation on which to write. Each day in their logs they record notes about Baylor and her illustrators. Some of the best thinking from students came in these entries. Scott wrote,

> When you read this book your eyes are on a constant roller coaster ride. If it's not the scattered words throughout the page, it's the sloping waves of earth that hide the clay fossils. . . . Did he copy

these [e.g., pictures of birds, lizards, and desert animals] off an old clay vase? I missed a lot of the small things when I looked the first time. . . . Reminds me of Norman Rockwell.

Charles wrote,

The illustrations in the book are very abstract. The desert sands are concocted in many shapes, forming a design more than a landscape. Many objects are the wrong size for their surroundings. The coyote's tracks dwarf the cactus on the ground yet the coyote is normal size. The gopher is a sleeping giant as people a tenth its size walk near the ground he's sleeping in. This characteristic is almost psychedelic while the sun is drawn so huge to give an idea of the climate.

Linda liked

the picture when you open the book *Celebration.* It reminds me of standing in a desert all alone overlooking the mountains and the valley just after the sunset. The clouds are as thick as cotton and the breeze smells as fresh as a new load of laundry. As the night begins to fall, I turn the page and find myself looking into a cave.

Reading log writing is more honest, real, and often more perceptive than other class work. I think when we say *composition* students freeze, their pencils turn to dead weight, and instead of thinking, wondering, and reacting, student writers force-write words into a foreign object they call a composition. They focus more on the formation of sentences and paragraphs, on the antecedent of pronouns, on penmanship, and on echoing whatever they think we as teachers want. These compositions often come in devoid of heartbeats. Real writers do not use lined white composition paper.

Another author I've used in shared experience is Farley Mowat. Since his books are longer, immersion takes more time, but by using sections from Mowat's books for discussions the students understand more of *A Whale for the Killing* (1972), *Never Cry Wolf* (1963), or *And No Birds Sang* (1979).

We also explore movies made of Mowat's books (*A Whale for the Killing* or *Never Cry Wolf*), video newscasts of trapped whales, magazines articles and newspaper reports on whaling, and library resources. These units take time to build but our schools are filled with resources; we just need to ask around. And like the integrated learning units students experience in elementary schools, this learning immersion appears to provide a wider base for learning and more variety to capture their learning soul. Nothing answers all the problems of our classrooms and no one technique reaches every student, but our job is to keep trying.

The students react to their reading of Mowat and his issues with a wide variety of responses including their own concerns about the environment. I like to think that these activities in our English classes will be remembered longer and called upon more frequently than the tedious exercises recommended by so many handbooks and study guides.

From these entries, students select an issue they care about as starters for longer essays or commentaries. Honest writing develops —students are freer to concentrate on ideas and not blinded by grades, mechanics, or handwriting. They know I'm reading for ideas and looking for risk taking and connections; they know they are talking to me and that I will respect their comments and I will write and talk back to them.

When I come across interesting entries, I either ask students to share them with the class or I record and read them aloud later as samples of good reading log writing and thinking. And always in these logs I find surprises—maybe not whole thoughts—that are quotable. Not every student will end up writing a tremendous paper, but every student writes gems and great lines in their logs. These lines are also excellent starting points for discussions or for longer pieces of writing such as these from freshman reading logs:

Hating the Yankees is as much a pastime as playing baseball.
Watch the logs crumble into the unforgiving fires.
There's no future in daydreaming.
No, Emily. How dreary to be nobody.
God didn't take time to make a nobody; he made everybody a some-
  body.
Like Kino, Sydney Carton shot his life away into a sea of death.
Sydney Carton and Kino both had dreams they knew would never come
  true.
Snow looks like popcorn popping with no cover to keep it down.

Other Ways to Reflect and Connect with Literature

Though reading logs are an excellent ongoing writing activity that engage students in thinking about their reading, there are other ways to reflect that offer variety and unique advantages.

Response sheets. Each day a different student is assigned the role of class secretary. The secretary listens to class discussion and synthesizes the talk and the class reactions. The response sheet should not be just a summary but should capture the feeling of the class that day. Creativity in design of the one-page response is encouraged along with artwork. The next day students bring their sheet to the office or library to make enough copies for each student and teacher in the class. (This aids in reviewing for students who have been absent.) The secretary for the day before starts the present class with the reading of her notes. The class can make corrections or suggestions, and unfinished business can be completed while today's secretary is busy at work. These dated sheets are kept in a folder by the students for use later in reviewing the literature unit or for studying for exams. On the other hand, these response sheets have drawbacks. They can get too competitive and cute rather than informative and fun. Some students need more help than others, and most need to be reminded of their need for clear handwriting.

Letters. Nancie Atwell documents this powerful technique in her classic *In the Middle* (1987). I use various options, such as letters written to another student in class commenting on concerns, issues, decisions within the book; or letters addressed to older or younger students who have agreed to respond, maybe even in a local college English methods class. It is important that letters be answered by someone, otherwise freshness wilts.

Poetry. Sometimes the best response to reading is writing a poem and expressing thoughts in a lyrical way. Poems can capture essences within the reading but may also curve off to follow new coastlines.

Personal narratives. As we talk about literature, members of the class may recall similar experiences and memories that happened to them or to someone in their circle of family and friends. In real-life reading, these are the heartbeats of book conversations. We need to teach our students that their personal responses, ending in personal narratives, are not only acceptable but encouraged, especially if the student writer can make a connection with the literature or can express the larger meaning beyond simple memory.

Free-choice responses. Teach the students that when they have something to say, part of their decision of what to say is deciding how to say it. Commentary, profiles like those in *People* or *The New Yorker,* field diaries, questionnaires, letters of recommendation, and questions for interviews are all valid choices. Have samples available so students can study these genres. Free-choice writing about literature should allow the students the same time and processes and feedback that we develop in our writing workshop classes, including time to brainstorm and try various leads, endings, discovery drafts, conferences, polishing, and sharing.

Thinking block. Stephen Marcus is a writer, computer expert, and innovative English writing teacher. His thinking block for literature—a Rubik's cube-like square—lets students see the variety of possibilities for writing and thinking about any reading.

Essay exams. I suppose we will never outgrow our need for essay exams on semester- and year-end tests. The best process I ever saw a teacher provide her students for writing excellent essay exams was in an advanced biology class. Pat Andruchuk did not try to find out everything her students didn't know but wanted to give them the opportunity to shine with their knowledge and understanding. After studying photosynthesis, she prepared the students for their essay test by writing the test question on the board. Then the class brainstormed possible topics and ideas needed to answer the question. They could ask her any question at all about the essay question and about photosynthesis and take notes on the discussion. During the next three days, students could come back after school or during lunch break or study halls for extra help through individual or small-group conferences. On their own time they were encouraged to reread references, take notes, and practice their essay answer. For ten minutes at the beginning of class each day, Pat continued to answer questions about photosynthesis. On the day of the exam, students could bring a one-page crib sheet—not the completed essay—filled with material they might use. The question was typed on a sheet and handed out to each student, who then wrote the essay. Pat said she had never received such terrific answers and exulted in the ability of the class.

Other ideas for daily writing encounters where students connect their thoughts and reactions with pieces of literature include writing

- a clarity statement: one sentence that unfolds a character, action, or theme
- open-ended questions—did something like this happen to you?
- a map of the character relationships within the book
- two or three questions per chapter
- abstracts, such as taking concepts like *good, bored,* or *war* and then making them concrete with specific details, often by using the senses or colors
- newspaper articles covering the period before the book starts, during the book's timeline, and after the book ends
- *New Yorker*-style stories and articles
- letters of recommendation for characters
- letters between characters
- questionnaires related to issues raised by the reading
- a character interview
- action scenes based on an action within a reading
- diary entries, either from the student, the point of view of a character, or an imaginary character within the reading
- split-entry sheets, with one column to record notes from the reading and the other to list questions. The left-hand column can also be used for questions formed before students read and the other column for answers from their research.

Always encourage students to choose their own way to reflect and connect with the literature.

Literature Selection

How do you decide what book to read next? recommendations from friends? browsing among the titles of your favorite author or genre? published reviews? You probably didn't think of assigned book reports. Few adults would ever read a book because they had to write a book report, take a quiz at the end of every chapter, or test the memory for minute details in a true-false test. Our reasons for pleasure reading have few connections to the reasons most schools give students for reading. Why is there such a gap between our own love for literature and what we promote in our English classrooms?

I once thought that I had to know every book the students read and would spend months getting prepared. After working closely with some elementary school teachers, I now know better. Karen Boettcher, a sixth-grade teacher, combines the elements that already work in her class with new ideas such as computer word processing, portfolios for self-evaluation, and multiple reading texts. Karen and her students explore reading and characters and writing in many ways, and from them I have learned to recognize the ability of readers to digest and furrow out poor, average, and excellent books.

While the classics are always valid reading, high school teachers also choose twentieth-century titles that relate more to today's stresses and struggles. Also have students read books you aren't familiar with but that have been recommended by librarians, teachers, or reading specialists who know your students and what that age level likes to read. Unfamiliar books will be more challenging and exciting for you. Imagine the freshness of your questions and the honesty of your predictions. You too will be a learner in the class, one of the students. With new books, students and teachers walk together through the wilds of unknown plots and tensions, and there excitement lurks.

WORKING WITH MAJOR NOVELS

Most students have had little experience reading complex adult novels, especially those with many substories that may not make sense until several parts have been pieced together. I call them jigsaw novels. Time and reflection may help to see and understand the beauty of the whole. A nearby art gallery displays a wonderful medieval tapestry that requires you to look closely and then stand back and see all of it. I tell students to use both their telescopic and wide-angle eye lens. Charles Dickens's *A Tale of Two Cities* demands a similar approach.

Dickens developed his characters from years of observations of people in London. *A Tale of Two Cities* is worth using as a mural in words whose layers students can peel off to see Dickens's accurate attention to color, shape, textures, symbols, foreshadowing, personification, digression, alliteration, and metaphors. Scenes stay with us: the spilled wine, the footsteps, the storm and the fire, storming the Bastille and the guillotine. The tapestry of this novel may at first seem overwhelming, but careful reading of specific passages enrich the whole novel. I would try not to beat this tool into a pulp, but seeing what one writer does can open doors to read pieces that might otherwise seem insurmountable to young readers.

An overnight or weekend homework assignment might be to ask students to think of authors they've read who have tried specific techniques seen in Dickens. Students record these books in their logs and then we share these discoveries orally. The results can range from Stephen King to Lois Duncan. It doesn't matter really whether the individual responses are all correct; it is the act of comparing, contrasting, and thus extending and connecting our readings that contains the merit.

One successful connection after finishing *Tale* is reading Shel Silverstein's *The Giving Tree* (1964). I ask students to *give* something at home and not announce it. This good deed could be washing and drying the dishes without being asked; babysitting a younger child with no payment; taking a younger brother or sister to the park, movie, or mall; reading to an elderly relative; or raking leaves. They are to just do it and then watch for reactions.

Many students were amazed at what happened. Parents wrote notes to me about the activity and the change in their teenager; even students saw parents in a new light. Unfortunately, some parents did not notice anything, but I try to get all students to participate in the class success of this activity.

If I gave the students a test at the end of *Tale*, it would be open-ended essay questions with students demonstrating what they know, not what they do not know. I want all students to be somewhat pleased at their reading of *Tale*. I used to give hundreds of little quotes for identification. Was the purpose to trick them up? Now I review characters through quotes during the reading so they will understand the purpose; I want them to keep the characters straight and to see Dickens's ability to draw individuals.

Writing about *Tale* is also important. I started out assigning the whole class the same writing topic. After a few years of unproductive, dull pieces, I tried to find what I was doing wrong. I realized my friends and family discuss readings all the time, but we seldom talk about the same element; we focus on different aspects within a book. Why shouldn't developing readers? My goal now is to get them to write and talk to me and others as they would naturally.

Some direct teaching is of course needed, such as how to find the elements they are responding to. We may brainstorm elements we can discuss, something like a reader's clinic. Our list might include sacrifice, the hatred of war, imprisonment, rebellion, revolution, mob psychology, revenge, love, giving, cities, or people caught in the middle of a dispute. As I also try to connect today's news with our literature, we may discuss war in Bosnia or revolution in Haiti. Literature should live.

MYTHOLOGY

Why study mythology today? Mythology is part of our language's heritage. Almost every day you can find an allusion to a Greco-Roman myth in newspapers, and sometimes South American, African, Native American, and Asian myths as well.

My goals in teaching mythology are students knowing the stories, gods, heroes, competitions, and love triangles and seeing the range of words, phrases, and anecdotes from myths that enhance their own communication skills. I concentrate on using the mythological terms in everyday writing and reading and give the students an example and ask what is meant by such allusions as the following: "Slim, wiry, and sharply handsome, my father still carried himself like the young soldier who had gone off in 1915 to fight the Great War, although he had come back from *Hades* with his right arm made useless by a German bullet" (Mowat 1979). I also have students answer questions that review their knowledge, including

Why is *Nike* a good name for sneakers and *Mercury* for a car?
DaVinci dreamed he was visited by Chiron. What do they have in common?
How is Thomas Edison a modern Prometheus?

In one class students just weren't getting the concept of myths, so one day I told them we would be collaborating on a play and their assignment was to name the characters for the roles listed on a sheet: telephone operator, movie director, basketball player, librarian, executive secretary, cook, senator, scientist, kindergarten teacher, doctor, dentist, tennis star, CEO, and president. As expected, they perpetuated stereotypes about the sex of certain jobs. Not one person gave a male name to the teacher or a female name to the CEO. The telephone operator, secretary, and librarian were all given female names. The scientist, senator, basketball player, and doctor were all male. Only the tennis player was given both male and female names. Then we discussed how they were contributing to the myths that certain jobs are for men and others for women. Once they engaged in talking about a myth they understood, whether they believed that myth or not, their engagement in classical mythology became more energetic.

Having students write their own myths following the same style and format of the myths we read is an exciting and often rewarding exercise. We brainstorm mysteries and unique natural features or events that we could use as our base for transformational myths:

white sand on beaches, Grand Canyon, different snowflake shapes, fog over the river, white buffalo, pine needles, ocean tides, woodpeckers, snow white not green or blue, moss on north side, blue flames becoming red, the Nile River flowing north, hee-hawing mules, jumping dolphins, and erupting geysers.

Depending on the ability and interest of each class, I like to expand their focus of Greek and Roman myths with a look at Nordic, English, and Celtic myths along with American folklore, tall tales, patriots, and superstars. Do we have heroes today? We would compile a list of possible heroes on the porcelain board and analyze our selections: actors, athletes, politicians, and so on. What is a media hero? Is a superstar naturally a hero? Is it a myth of sports that winning is everything? What does a person have to do to be a hero? Are there anonymous heroes? The more thoughtful the class, the more lively our discussions become. The science of arguing orally is a skill that often translates into powerful compositions.

What qualities would a hero need? Our list usually includes honesty, strength, good intentions, a tragic flaw or emotional weakness, the desire to prove oneself, pride, great adversity, athleticism, and respect. In classes that did not study many myths, we might do a survey based on our reading of heroes:

Of all men/women living or dead, who could be a hero?
What female/male historical figure would you like to have known?
What author would you like to write your own story?
What author would you most like to meet?
If you were to train for a sporting event, which athlete would you like to train you?
If marriages were arranged in America, which historical figure would you want your parents to arrange for you to marry?
With whom would you change places for a day?
If you were president, who would you pick as vice president?

As you can see, these questions get students thinking of their own attitudes and dreams while allowing each person to participate and succeed.

SHAKESPEARE

What is it we are trying to accomplish in reading Shakespeare's plays? Interestingly enough, schools often choose among the least powerful of his works for study, notably *Julius Caesar* and *Romeo and*

Juliet. Though these two plays can introduce the style and form of a Shakespearean play, they should only be the beginning for new readers of tragedies and comedies. Our job is to help students see why reading the classics—and Shakespeare in particular—is a valuable activity that they have a right to do (whether they want to or not).

Shakespeare offers versatility (histories, comedies, and tragedies) and universal themes (love, fear, greed, power, jealousy). His skill in portraying characters in words is unsurpassed. Who else has created a vacillating man like Hamlet? A woman of wild ambition as Lady Macbeth? The unforgettable Falstaff, Bottom, Puck, Brutus, Malvolio? His plays are filled with conflict, misidentification, bad timing, confusion, love, and rivalry. Action surges in his plays. And as Ben Jonson said, Shakespeare understood human nature. The reasons are there to read Shakespeare's plays, but how can we ignite his fire in students?

Most grade seven and eight teachers select either *Romeo and Juliet* or *Julius Caesar* as their introduction to Shakespearean drama. The former is more popular, but *Julius Caesar* is actually easier to introduce as its language is more direct and uses fewer images, metaphors, and allusions.

Students keep logs as we unfurl his plays, with one page each devoted to the man himself, the Globe Theater, the meaning of tragedy, themes, setting, and important drama terms, along with a page for each of the major characters. Students take on the role of one major or important minor character and follow that person, rereading those lines and recording reactions, comments, and questions. I might also use a few directed questions for students to consider: Could a world filled with Hamlets exist? Did Caesar deserve to die? How are Romeo and Huck alike? How is Willy Loman like Lear?

We practice several scenes aloud, trying to get into the character (I have sometimes shown a sample read-through of the M*A*S*H actors as they rehearse). Plays are meant to be seen, so line-by-line silent reading misuses Shakespeare's plays.

I also ask the same questions we do of other writers. Why is the first scene first? What is the dramatic function of the servants starting the fight between the Capulets and Montagues?

As they read, guiding questions help students understand sections: Why does the Friar agree to marry the two? I want a tight reading of certain sections and I want students to grasp Elizabethan language and lyric poetry. Shakespeare's plays offer wonderful opportunities for students to see so many dramatic techniques in full action. And once a student explores the beauty of Shakespeare, many other plays seem approachable.

Culminating activities on a full-length play might include a student newspaper based on the stories and events, a modern interpretation of a scene, seeing plays in person, and surveys asking who Shakespeare "was" and if he wrote these plays.

EXPLORING POETRY

I read poetry but until recently I never wrote poetry and I was always in awe of those who did. I taught Awe of Poetry. This somehow didn't go over very well. But I charged ahead, making every student compose a poem or two. The results were usually beyond bad, falling into the realm of vile, sour, and stagnant. Why couldn't my students write poetry?

At a workshop on some other long-forgotten topic, a speaker said sometimes the fault is not the students' but the instructor's. So I put away my college anthologies and sought poems my students would savor. During a unit on language, I started reading some of these poems aloud under the guise of word play and words in action. I didn't think much about this reading until the first day of a literature unit when students said, "You forgot to read one of those word things today." With an invitation like this, I grabbed a book from the shelf and read. From then on I read a poem a day (except during writing units, when the whole period is spent working on writing). Often I would write it on the chalkboard, leaving the book around for students to explore on their own. Our favorites include *Old Possum Book of Practical Cats,* John Donne, Carl Sandburg, anything by Frost, e. e. cummings, Edwin Hoey, Robert Francis, Karl Shapiro, Gerard Manley Hopkins, and Theodore Roethke. Other poets to offer students include Nikki Giovanni, Marge Piercy, Mary Oliver, Seamus Heaney, Cynthia Rylant, and Paul Janeczka.

My students learn poems, design posters with poems as the focus, and include poems in their multigenre reports. And we read, sometimes several during one period. Out of this came some fine poetry written by the students, often from their readings of novels and plays. I try to read poems with joy, leaving my awe in my college notes. Now poetry appears for every unit and theme.

THEME UNITS

Carefully thought-out theme units can establish a higher level of independence while integrating the curriculum. If we want to read literature pieces in a theme motif, then we need to search out available materials. For a war and literature theme in a senior class, I found a whole set of slides, filmstrips, and art reprints on the mythology of war in many cultures.

As a class we first read Stephen Crane's *Red Badge of Courage,* looked at Henry Fleming's different views of war, and explored war poetry from Walt Whitman, Rupert Brook, Wilfred Owen, Henry Reed, and E. E. Cumming.

Students selected another book—either fiction or nonfiction—to read on their own. We looked at the Civil War through diaries and newspaper reprints. In one fast-moving class, we looked at the changing views of war heroes in mythology: *Beowulf,* Chaucer's "Knights' Tale," *Le Morte d'Arthur, Trolius and Criseyda, Idylls of the King, Don Quixote, Henry IV, Henry V,* and *Julius Caesar.* Student readings included Hemingway's *A Farewell to Arms,* and *For Whom the Bell Tolls,* Heller's *Catch 22,* Hershey's *Hiroshima,* Remarque's *All Quiet on the Western Front, Dispatches* by Michael Herr, and *Things They Carried* by Tim O'Brien.

Students get a new vision when they view war in art. The "Art in War" issue of *Art and Man* magazine is excellent. Photography, first used extensively in the Civil War tell dramatic stories. David Douglas Duncan's Vietnam photos demand reactions. We also examined war through the brilliance of the short films *Chickamauga* and *Occurrence at Owl Creek Bridge.*

We discussed how war in music changed over the centuries, including the patriotic "Battle Hymn of the Republic" to "Bangladesh" by George Harrison, John Denver's "The Box," and Buffy Sainte-Marie's haunting "Universal Soldier." We read short books such as *Rose Blanche, Faithful Elephants, The Wall,* and my favorite little book, *Fifty-seven Reasons Not to Have a Nuclear War* by Marty Asher.

When a unit like this is finished your students have read a variety of literature, experienced a topic in depth, and seen firsthand how art, music, history, literature, and critical and creative thinking are all interrelated. And they get an opportunity to begin to examine where they stand on important issues.

Planning a Theme Unit

First, consider what you hope to gain from an integrated unit. Is the purpose clear to you? If it isn't, then the unit will be muddled to your students. I also ask myself if the learning will be better in a theme unit.

If I can give positive responses, then I go ahead and plan. I am a collector, so my way of building a unit is to collect items and ideas over time. I do this long before the unit will be presented. This is one reason I like to have an overview from day one that gives a general direction for the year while allowing me to adjust to learning styles and class differences.

A week before the unit I review my material. I like to list so I know what I have and can see where there are holes. And the simple act of listing opens up my mind to other possibilities and connections. I develop this list further by having columns labeled art, music, film, photography, speakers, readings, writing, history, science, math, and miscellaneous. These columns remind me of what to consider as well as visually indicating strong and weak subtopics. I learned this type of across-the-curriculum outlining from my friends Judy and Bill Egan. It is a clear, effective device for providing information on curriculum connections.

A few days before the unit, I sort out material, select the areas in which I can best maneuver, ask for information from librarians and teachers who use theme units, and reread books that suggest further extensions. In other words, I begin to teach myself, to work with the documents, and to ground myself in more knowledge than I need for the unit. A deep foundation allows me to offer the students a free-flowing and unforced unit. When I taught day to day, I was unprepared for the flow of students' thinking and questions. By arming myself, I can follow the students' lead and let their interests and curiosity determine the actual class outline—within each class. But you never know what to expect. When the unexpected happens, and it always does, I invite students to find the answers.

Next I think of the best way to present the material to each group of students. I tentatively outline a possible sequence that is logical to me. During this time, I look for an introduction. As in writing, the lead in to a unit is vital and often establishes the tone, direction, and success or failure of the whole unit. If possible and reasonable, I try to find a connection to the students' life and to today's world. Where does this unit fit? Why would they bother learning through this theme? Does this theme have a universal quality? What does it all add up to?

Can I find a quote, passage, poem, or other connection to something they already have mentioned or questioned? If not, then I select what appears to be my strongest piece of the puzzle and use it as a lead, varying by class. For instance, in a mythology unit I might use a quote comparing Jim Henson to Zeus in one class while in another I might ask students if they have been told stories that explain mysteries in nature. In another class—perhaps one with less prior knowledge—I might do an oral story telling of one of the more vivid transformational myths, perhaps the one about Ceres asking Neptune for help with the harvest. Neptune then jokes around by first making a camel, hippo, and giraffe, before finally creating the hard-working horse. "Do any of you have teasing brothers like Neptune? How do you react? Why do they tease? Are any of you those teasing older brothers or sisters?" The stories that they subsequently tell are myths of their families and oral history like the myths of ancient Greece and Rome.

In other classes, I may ask students about the Olympics and where that name and tradition came from or ask them about Greece and its origins, using a map of the Mediterranean as a prop. (I have been lucky to have many first-generation Greek children in my classes and they bring an extraordinary depth of knowledge about their culture.) All of these devices are valid elements to integrate into each class over the unit. I might also have a list of topics, readings, and assignments I definitely want to explore. I will want students to do reading and research on their own, including reading other versions of their chosen myth, reading myths from other cultures, and examining heroes. I know I will have the students try creating a transformational myth, a modern labor of Hercules, and an oral presentation of their research. I know all this before I begin, though everything is flexible. The only thing that is not flexible is our study of mythology as our birthright.

But how all this develops varies as each class evolves. I do not worry about staying together. Teaching just isn't that neat. In teaching there are no laminated lesson plans. That's why over the years I do write a list of possible topics and themes to include, but I leave a lot of room for change to be able to appreciate the individuality of each group of learners and to follow their lead.

LITERATURE AND WRITING

Writing in secondary school literature classes today is too frequently intended only for testing; it's mostly assigned rather than taught and involves little feedback. Credit is given for the absence of error, for fancy words, and for the regurgitation of lectures. Students mostly write *about* literature—book reports and those almighty analytical essays that end up being a surface analysis.

Or the writing takes the form of ambiguous assignments like "analyze the poem" or "write a character sketch about a character," a character that has been too-little discussed. Assignments without direct and indirect teaching lead to tedious writing for the student and tedious reading for the teacher who then corrects tediously. This is not real-life writing: it is not writing to learn.

A double standard exists in writing for English classes: "creative" writing is fun, filled with drama, tension, surprise, and challenges, but writing about literature is dull: analysis, outlining, summarization, and review. In all the years I've been behind or in front of the big desk, none of my students went on to become literary analysis writers, critics, reviewers, or writers of the boring blurbs in reference books. We have to upgrade writing about literature.

Though we know more now about student learning styles, much of this knowledge has not affected our teaching of literature. We still indoctrinate and ask students to rehash class notes, and choose literature by some cultural catalog. Our major role in literature, Langer (1992) says, should be intellectual development.

Writing can help students achieve intellectual development and literacy. Writing can help students learn literature and think about and understand the language and stories of others. Writing can help students make connections between what students know (prior knowledge and experience) and new knowledge gained from reading, listening, talking, arguing, and viewing. Writing helps to narrow the distance between the words on the page and the student reader's understanding.

We want our students to stretch and grow, not just parrot what they have read or—worse—what we have told them to think about a particular reading. Students do not need to read or hear literary analysis before they read a piece of literature; they need to explore what they like, why they like it, how it connects to what they already know, and how the author offers new insights and challenges. Remember the old assignment line: Write an original short story with the elements of royalty, religion, sex, and mystery. The joke ends with one student finishing in just a few minutes by writing, "My God! The Queen is pregnant. Who did it?"

We need to replace the once-a-marking-period assigned writing with shorter and more frequent writing in which students have to engage reading with their own thoughts and with the blank page. Beginning writers need daily engagement to connect with new ideas and insights.

We need to ask questions that stretch the reading: "Did something like this ever happen to you?" In *Huck Finn,* why did Twain choose this strange ending? We need to make them think and make connections; we need to teach what elements constitute a character sketch, review, or editorial.

Books like *Summer of My German Soldier* by Betty Greene offer students insights on issues they deal with: being an outcast and feeling alone and lonely. Did you ever feel like this or do you know someone who does? And Greene explores many other topics as well. All of these can be discussed, probed, and written about while illuminating the piece of literature in a way that makes it part of the student's knowledge base.

We need to eliminate the traditional book report. Students write great book reports by the third and fourth grades, so we should offer them activities more challenging and meaningful. Ken Goodman says that we not only learn to read by reading and write by writing but we also learn to read by writing and write by reading. By the time students get to junior and senior high, time should be provided for them to understand literature by writing.

LITERATURE AS WRITING

We send students into a talespin when we consider literature as something removed from their lives, something to respect, appreciate, and dissect. It is more useful to view the literature we read as examples of writers at work. With this approach, we can point to effective word selections, phrases, and leads. For instance, if the whole class just read *Red Badge of Courage, To Kill a Mockingbird,* or *Cold Sassy Tree,* go back to the beginning and reread the first section. Why did the author open the book this way? The discussion helps them later when they evaluate individual readings.

In Chaucer's Prologue to the *Canterbury Tales,* I point out the power of the one-liner. The students can try composing their own one-liners with the ultimate goal of using this device in their writing. Here are sample one-liners written by freshmen:

He's the kind of dog who would chew nails just to look tough.
He's the type of person who always put more wood on the fire.
He was like our old car—everyday there would be a new problem.
Tom is the kind of guy who could tell a bad joke and you wouldn't know it.

She hates her new shoes 'til someone else likes them.
Her life consisted of nieces and nephews and Thursday morning shopping sprees.

When given time to think, ask questions, brainstorm, and draft, students can achieve excellent results. What happens too often is we as instructors forget the reason for writing essays—or attribute the reason to be earning a grade and lose sight of the goals of learning and growing.

For a list of suggested readings, see Appendix, page 133.

PICTURE BOOKS WITH OLDER STUDENTS

Picture books are a treasure trove of reading and writing connections. Thousands of outstanding picture books have been published, many by extraordinary writers. These books offer English classes other dimensions of literature and writing to explore as well as design.

Why use them? These books are quick to read and reread. Students get to see stories in shorter forms, with the development more clearly identifiable. In one class period we can read an entire story—beginning, middle, and end—talk about it, reread it, and still have time for other activities. We can't do this with novels and plays on the regular reading list. Picture books are inexpensive so you could get one or more for each student in the class. Within the genre there is extensive variety, ranging from the innovative alphabet books of Jerry Pallotta, the ecological concerns of Lynne Cherry, to the natural wonders of Seymour Simon.

Will your students take to using picture books? If you have a positive attitude they will. If you really do not believe in what you are doing, students see that in a wink. So look over some picture books and see what they offer. I've already mentioned doing a unit with Byrd Baylor and illustrator Peter Parnell; my students at that time were juniors in a college composition class. Look at *Brown Angels* by Walter Dean Myers as extension of your reading of black writers or *Rose Blanche* by Roberto Innocenti when you read *Diary of Anne Frank*. For an awareness of language, read the vivid images of Cynthia Rylant's personal narrative stories of *Appalachia: Voices of Sleeping Birds. Snowed In* by Barbara Lucas is a great survival story. Comparing the various books by a single author such as Eve Bunting can be very fruitful. If you want to develop or expand creative thinking read *Math Curse* by Jon Scieszka. Be selective. Some picture books—like any other genre—are frivolous and insulting to readers. Leave those on the store shelf. Set up diverse types of reading early in the class: bring in newspapers, magazines, catalogs, and music cassette and disk liners as examples of good writing. Next to this the picture books will look natural. Teach students to seek good reading and writing all around. Finally, give them time to read in your class. When reading Byrd Baylor I set aside entire class periods and invite the students to read as many of her books as they can, taking notes on what they saw and read.

Picture books need to be read aloud with verve: speak up, change voices, and practice. Nothing can destroy a good picture book more than a bland reading. For practice, try *Charlie Parker Played Be Bop* by Chris Raschka. And if you are at a reading or writing convention, check out the children's book authors reading their own work. I didn't really understand *Koala Lou* until I heard the author—Mem Fox—read it aloud.

For a list of picture books to use with specific themes, see Appendix, page 141.

FOR FURTHER READING

Andrasick, Kathleen. 1993. *Opening Texts: Using Writing to Teach Literature.* Portsmouth, NH: Heinemann.

Atwell, Nancie. 1987. *In the Middle.* Portsmouth, NH: Boynton/Cook.

Atwell, Nancie, ed. 1989. *Workshop 1: Writing and Literature.* Portsmouth, NH: Heinemann.

Baylor, Byrd. 1986. *I'm in Charge of Celebrations.* New York: Charles Scribner's Sons.

Benedict, Susan, and Lenore Carlisle, eds. 1992. *Beyond Words.* Portsmouth, NH: Heinemann.

Braided Lives: An Anthology of Multicultural American Writing. 1991. Saint Paul: Minnesota Humanities Commission.

Day, Frances Ann. 1994. *Multicultural Voices in Contemporary Literature: A Resource for Teachers.* Portsmouth, NH: Heinemann.

Graves, Donald. 1992. *Explore Poetry.* Portsmouth, NH: Heinemann.

Greene, Bette. 1973. *Summer of My German Soldier.* New York: Dial Press.

Harwayne, Shelley. 1994. *Lasting Impressions.* Portsmouth, NH: Heinemann.

Heard, Georgia. 1989. *For the Good of the Earth and Sun: Teaching Poetry.* Portsmouth, NH: Heinemann.

Hughes, Ted. 1986. *Poetry in the Making.* London: Faber and Faber.

Janeczko, Paul, ed. 1983. *Poetspeak.* New York: Collier.

Kaywell, Joan F., ed. 1993. *Adolescent Literature as a Complement to the Classics.* Norwood, MA: Christopher-Gordon Publishers.

Langer, Judith A. 1992. "Rethinking Literature Instruction." In *Literature Instruction: A Focus on Student Response,* edited by Judith A. Langer. Urbana, IL: NCTE.

———. Nd. *A New Look at Literature Instruction.* New York: McDougal, Littell.

Lindberg, Gary. 1986. "Coming to Words: Writing as Process and the Teaching of Literature." In *Only Connect: Uniting Reading and Writing,* edited by Thomas Newkirk. Portsmouth, NH: Boynton/Cook.

Merriam, Eve. 1986. *A Sky Full of Poems.* New York: Dell.

Mowat, Farley. 1963. *Never Cry Wolf.* New York: Houghton Mifflin.

———. 1972. *A Whale for the Killing.* New York: Houghton Mifflin.

———. 1979. *And No Birds Sang.* New York: Houghton Mifflin.

———. 1993. *Born Naked.* New York: Houghton Mifflin.

Newkirk, Tom. 1986. *Only Connect: Uniting Reading and Writing.* Portsmouth, NH: Boynton/Cook.

O'Reilly, Mary Rose. 1993. *The Peaceable Classroom.* Portsmouth, NH: Boynton/Cook.

Probst, Robert. *Response and Analysis: Teaching Literature in Junior and Senior High School.* Portsmouth, NH: Boynton/Cook.

Rief, Linda. 1991. *Seeking Diversity: Language Arts with Adolescents.* Portsmouth, NH: Heinemann.

———. 1994. Threads of Life: Reading, Writing, and Music. *Voices from the Middle* 1 (1): 18–25.

Rosenblatt, Louise. 1938. *Literature as Exploration.* New York: Appleton-Century.

Silverstein, Shel. 1964. *The Giving Tree.* New York: Harper & Row.

Tchudi, Stephen. 1991. *Planning and Assessing the Curriculum in English Language Arts.* Alexandria, VA: Association for Supervision and Curriculum Development.

Whaley, Liz, and Liz Dodge. 1993. *Weaving in the Women: Transforming the High School English Curriculum.* Portsmouth, NH: Heinemann.

5
Writing Ideas, Strategies, and Guides

Writing is like driving in a foreign country: You have a sense of where you are going but it is still new and unrelenting in its surprises.

—student

Several years ago I took a photography class. Our first assignment was to bring in the best pictures we had already taken. The instructor looked at my water reflection of a neon rainbow dinghy. "Good. Now, where are the other pictures you took at the same time?" I hadn't. I had taken only that one. He shook his head. "Too bad." I've gone back to that same spot and even found the same boat, but I've never been able to capture the light in the same way.

I learned from that one photograph to look at things from different angles, to not be satisfied with just the first view, but to move around and seek combinations and patterns. Like photography, teaching isn't one step after the other.

Since writing is not easy, it figures that the teaching of writing is not easy. Where do students go after they have started to write? What am I doing in the class as the students write? How do I keep the writing going all year? I will discuss some common questions and topics of concern.

WHY EMPHASIZE WRITING?

Original thinking flourishes with writing. The student cannot just sit passively; the student must act and react. Students begin to see the power and beauty of words by constructing with words. They look at common things in an uncommon way. They become sensitive to ordinary and real experiences. Their interest in reading and in literature increases as they read each other's writing. Writing shows students the rhythms of their own language and how language changes for different audiences. Students want to express their opinions, reactions, and attitudes, and they have a right to know how to make meaning and communicate clearly.

HOW DO YOU START THE SECOND WRITING UNIT?

During the last three days of a literature unit, I remind students to start searching for a writing topic. The teacher's attitude is important here. I am always excited—really—and I want them to know this. I like reading their papers and I like having them work through their subjects to craft interesting papers.

Often I start the second writing unit with copies of good pieces from the last unit. I never call them the "best," just papers that reach readers. In each class there are students who never make a mechanical mistake and write perfectly boring papers. If I select the paper with the top grades all the time, it may be written by the same person. I want the seed papers to include as many student writers as possible over the year as well as some of the most interesting papers. I also look for papers that show hard work, that reach for potential, and accept a challenge.

These papers demonstrate the writer's attempt at some skill such as dialogue, metaphor, or flashback. Even just solid active verbs and strong well-constructed sentences need to be shown. We read these papers out loud. Sometimes the students just listen, but other times I provide them with copies to mark up and circle favorite parts. I want them to know that not all parts of a text are created equally and to identify those words and phrases that really say something. We talk about these papers and ask the authors what they did to reach this level of writing. It isn't often that beginning writers have the opportunity to talk to writers directly, so this is an important and valuable activity. As the beginning, it sets the tone for working and striving. Should you try talking about published writing as well? I used model papers by professionals until one student said to me, "I hate those. They make me believe I will never reach that level. If student papers were used then we have a chance."

This opening to a new writing unit varies somewhat because now each class is clearly different with different needs that I try to respect. I keep good records so at the beginning of this unit I read them over and make flexible plans for what I want to accomplish within the overall goal of improved writing and a better understanding of how to go about writing.

The first few days in a new unit are similar, with one or two days of exercises (if needed), brainstorming and collecting details and then writing as soon as students enter class. Some days end with a clinic, but the main goal is to get students writing. Move around the room to check questions, concerns, and problems, and then stop and sit and write yourself. Let them see you start, stop, stare, cross out, write hurriedly, slowly, whatever. Your body language is information to them.

Also in this unit I introduce peer conferences. Students know each other a bit better by the second unit and I have a good idea of which students will work supportively with each other. Some students have peer edited before, but I still like to introduce my way, which I hope lasts longer than lecturing and giving directions.

One class of freshmen I recall was made up of especially avid writers, probably because they had failed in other language arts activities. One girl wrote pages and pages on everything she could remember about her boyfriend, sort of an unfocused "all about" paper that primary teachers use.

I gave a workshop on focus using the target approach narrowing on the bulls-eye topic, but it didn't influence her; Kris just had too much to decipher her focus herself. I asked if she would read the paper to two other girls in the class, though these three students had only known each other for about a month. The four of us sat together; I asked them to trust and help each other as conference partners and offer Kris suggestions on how to focus. They listened with the sincerity of their charge. I don't know if it was the trust I placed in them or a chemistry that would have been there anyway, but these three girls turned out to be the best peer conference students I've ever had, even counting my top-level classes (Kearns 1996).

Other ways I start off a new writing unit include distributing a handout of leads from the last set of papers, with examples of the great, the workable, and the really forgettable leads but using no names. And we discuss why some are better than others. After this brief introduction, the students write the rest of the period. They understand "write" can mean to search for a subject, list possible titles, quick write on leads, make a discovery draft, cast a quick summary or outline, draw or blueprint ideas, and reread items in logs or folders to find subjects. I don't want talking as students should begin writing independently.

Joanne Coughlin, a junior-high teacher and friend, is successful with a different routine: she wants her students to discuss their pre-writing topics and instructs them to conference immediately after they locate a topic. Their partner listens and asks questions about where the new topic might be going. This same partner stays with the writer all through the writing of that paper from topic selection to publication. Coughlin provides several conference areas around her room and her students' talk becomes fuel for writing.

Each day I do a status check—at first in front of the whole class—as a teaching tool so they learn about their responsibility and other options for work. Students do not always know what constitutes writing time, so the status check and my writing circle help to define how they can manage their time. Later, I check each student individually as a troubleshooter and to record information specific to that student.

During these days, students write. As their coach, I help them *during* the writing and not just after the essential work is finished. I try to move around the room randomly (otherwise students in the last row will know you are not getting to them today). I try to read their body language and to encourage them to focus on their writing.

As they get into the writing and revising and conferencing, I tell them to come right in each day and get working. When they come to class those days, I am already in conference with an early student or I am writing at a student desk with my folder. I model the behavior I expect from them that day. I like to sit at a student desk if one is available because they think it is easier to write at the big desk. Students can always use the big desk if they want, but I want to demonstrate that I will struggle with the size of the students' desk, which was never designed with writers in mind. If I had my choice I would have clipboards for students to take to their corners and large worktables to spread out writing in progress. But I seldom am offered choices in regard to rooms or desks or space.

My goal is to get the students to know the processes of writing. I want them to recognize topics they can handle and how to approach the writing of these topics. For this I use as many before-composing exercises as I feel are necessary for the class or groups within the class. These will not be individually graded. We're priming the writing pump.

Murray (1985) says predrafting time is the period for writers to search, select, collect, focus, and rehearse. He offers many ways to collect and generate subtopics: brainstorming, drawing, thinking, interviewing, drawing, discussions, observations, journal writing, mapping, rereading, conferencing, listening, talking, and collecting topic lists in a folder. I like to publish a list of topics used by students last semester so others can see the possibilities.

These early composing activities build confidence. Students see they can recognize and write about an idea. Prewriting stimulates thought and gives students a start. More prewriting time is needed if the students have not been writing or when they delve into a new genre. Like artist sketches, prewriting gets them to rehearse off-stage and to mull ideas over before they lock up a piece.

Prewriting can be exercises in thinking and observing. With classes who recognize irony, I introduce Ken Macrorie's fabulous realities (1984), surprises and oddities in everyday life. After students share their own fabulous realities, we discuss how, when, and where these could be used in a writing piece. One student wrote about weird road signs in our state: Frost Heaves, No-Salt Area, Eat Here and Get Gas. He once saw Your Tax Money at Work near highway construction workers milling around. Another student saw a sign for a monastery followed by a highway sign telling all to Enter Here. A local restaurant billboard read All You Can Eat Buffet. Help Wanted. At an intersection near housing for the elderly is a sign: Caution. Dear Crossing. My favorite fabulous reality is the highway sign near the entrance to a very prestigious private school: Slow Students.

Open-Ended Questions

Besides a writing folder, my students keep a writing log. For this I find it easier to use a three-ringed binder that the traditional blue books or stitched notebooks. Before the year starts I check all the outlets in town for the best three-ring binder prices and most students then buy their own. I buy extras for students who can't afford any price. I requisition a three-hole punch every year but never receive one, so I buy paper with holes; college-ruled paper looks more serious than the wide-ruled school paper. At a college bookstore, I also get the half-lined and half-blank sheets of paper in the law or science sections for observation activities that includes drawing. Our duplication center now makes copies on three-holed paper for handouts.

For the writing notebook I give open-ended questions. I tell students to take those questions and think, stretch, and strain. I recommend that they let ideas flow and piggyback, that they not worry about connections; this is practice. If they are hot and heavy into a topic of their own, they can use it. My question is just a suggestion but I do want everyone writing fast and filling at least one page. Some open-ended questions that work for me and my students:

What place has a special meaning to you?
What place offers special sounds for you?
What place has special rhythms all its own?
Is there a photo, painting, or timely detail that says more than others?
What family ritual is important to you?
What gesture or object clearly identifies a family member?
What experience happened in only three minutes but still has strong
    effects?
What person do you care most about?
What really old clothes will you never throw out?
What do you really like or dislike?
What does weather do for you? to you?

This last question is especially effective right after a big weather event. I have even stopped class so we can look out at a storm approaching. In one class the chairs were lined up looking west and we often saw a blizzard or downpour coming. We would stop and watch. Then I would ask if anyone wanted to write about the storm. What did it look like? How did it make you feel? What words can we use to describe what we saw? What does the snow (or rain) mean to us? Farley Mowat's description of arctic snow from *The Snow Walkers* is an especially appropriate reading.

I never, ever give the ridiculous topics listed in grammar books such as "describe your favorite month." Fifteen year olds do not have a favorite month. Old people who write those grammar books have favorite months. I also join in and try each exercise myself. This also helps me to understand and evaluate my questions. They see me start and stop, get a whirl, and write fast for two minutes, which helps them understand that writing is not easy for anyone, even English teachers. Remember instead that these activities are exercises and stretches. Some may lead to a longer paper, but others are left as part of the developing writers' portfolio of attempts. After we've done a few exercises—say five or six—I ask students to go back and look them over for a key element, focus, or thread that could be developed into a longer piece of writing. Whether these are used as springboards to longer pieces is not as important as the search through the students' list of possibilities.

Milking a Subject

I used to tell students they could write about the same subject only once. Now I imagine telling Robert Frost, "All right, no more of those farm poems; get real," or saying to James Michener, "Enough with the long historical novels! Try a mystery or an epic poem." As teachers we often separate students from a subject they really like and know something about.

I did not realize this until I started to write myself. I like to write what I can do best and am most interested in doing: informational and travel pieces, but no fiction and few poems. Write with your students and you will learn more than any book or course or lecture can provide. Would you send your child to a piano teacher who said, "Oh no. I don't play. I just teach"?

Milk a subject, I tell students at this stage. If they really have something to write about, they should stay with it. And I show them how to milk a subject by walking all around it. I may use a photography analogy here (I keep my rainbow boat photo next to my desk as a reminder). A photographer, for instance, might take a whole roll of pictures on one subject, looking for textures, colors, shapes, details, and different angles. When I freelanced, a camera company once gave me and four other photographers ten rolls apiece, telling us to just take everything Chris Evert did. I learned if a subject is worth photographing, it is worth photographing well and often.

Why not do the same with a subject that excites a student writer? Write a piece on the who, what, where, when, why, and how of something. Look at all these questions and determine what is possible. Or look at different genres. Write a piece of fiction, then a letter sequence, then an interview. These attempts will narrow the subject and also organize and distinguish pieces for information. Only a few students will actually try three or four pieces on the same topic, but all students like the freedom to have that choice.

Often student writers submit papers that already contain two or more stories, which provides a natural transition to a clinic on milking a subject. I do, however, mention that if the first paper is weak then the next one must be dramatically better.

From Making Lists to Stockpiling

Listing is like slow, controlled brainstorming. Listing is most effective after students know how to brainstorm and have selected a topic. It is especially good for building an authority list. Everyone is an authority on something. No one knows about your dog more than you, at least not in this class, so I have students make a list of things they are authorities on. I do mine too: Hampton Beach, tennis, Ireland, the West Side, Italian restaurants in Boston, photography, football, lobstering, playing on the beach as a kid, shrimp dip, Notre Dame, mysteries, Connemara ponies, sea glass, Myzachy.

We then share and check any challenges. Several students may list football, the Grateful Dead, or snowmobiling, and we challenge each other with questions. The last one standing—figuratively—is the class authority. I love this process because it develops the real feeling of authority when students can stand up and defend their knowledge. I get involved too and they love beating me (but I do know a lot about football).

The next step is to select one topic from the authority list and brainstorm, map, or discovery draft everything we can think about on this subject. Again I do one example, perhaps on the overhead with the light off. From my list I select "playing on the beach as a kid" and start writing words and phrases associated with it:

hunting for starfish, crabs, minnows, periwinkles
Sunday in whites
seaweed fights
how to eat lobster
front porches
rain/lightning storms
Somerville, Mass. friends
license plate game
McCarthy house
hurricanes
games to play on the beach
beach baseball
grape leaves

Are these all part of one paper or are there several papers here? I want students to see the difference between information lists and an actual subject for a focused paper. Beach baseball is probably a separate story, while I could do a paper on all the games we invented to take up our days on the beach. Is there a paper here? Maybe two papers? I think aloud to prime their own collecting and selecting.

Another prewriting activity that sometimes works is listing people of interest, though this activity doesn't go too far if the names start at Bon Jovi and end with a Power Ranger. You'll have to judge whether this just becomes part of the folder or an active jumping off into a writing piece. This list can also be referred to later when we explore character sketches or personality profiles.

Another good brainstorming list is "Things I Want to Know More About." This list also reinforces that wanting to know more is good. We follow up this activity with time on the CD-ROM encyclopedia to help them extend their curiosity. Whether the interest is in outer space or John F. Kennedy or panda bears, the visual connection with new technologies can't help but make students more inquisitive and willing to search. Whether or not this search leads to a paper is secondary right now. It's the search itself and the attitude that will last longer. (Now we can add the internet to the search as well as other computer disks.)

After searching for a subject but before writing a draft, I need to stockpile information to help me focus. I share this information and teach students to stockpile information by collecting lists, phrases, ads, sentence outlines, random jottings, sensory descriptions, comparisons, titles, experiences, leads, interviews, notes, drawings, random thoughts, daydreams, and piggyback ideas.

With this technique I want students to slow down and think as they prepare to write. I tell them I stockpile all the time, especially if I already know information and do not want to forget anything. After they write lists of words and phrases, then we try opening sentences and lead-ins. We stop and look for a quote, metaphor, or anecdote. By making them stop, I hope to offer them other ingredients for developing details, for showing and not just telling.

Shared Experiences

Giving students some common experience allows them to share, compare, contrast, and discuss that experience. We often do this in literature as we may all read and discuss one book, but the same foundation is needed in writing—and for the same reasons. We expand our discussion when we have a common hook. Shared experiences can include reading a poem, seeing a short film, viewing an art exhibit, hearing a speaker, or comparing how a major news event is covered in several newspapers. I try to use current events as much as possible, but I also keep a folder filled with other possibilities.

After experiencing the event, students write a response on any aspect, minute or major. I look for immediate reactions. When shared, students see the variety of responses and understand that this variety is expected and accepted and can open them to talking about literature, art, or other subjects. The shared experience provides the whole class with a common point of departure and reference.

Shared experiences break the attitude that the teacher has the right answer and the students' job is to try and find that answer. I construct shared experiences several times a year, especially at the beginning of the class. Before the event, I give students some idea of what they are to see and review with them how to prepare for reaction writing: get an overview, go back and look closely, stand in close, stand back, read any liner notes, take your own notes, look for what strikes you most, and try to see strengths and weaknesses. We talk about what we experience and then sit and write responses. Just as the class is ending, we share. Students work on their reflections that night to share the next day.

Each student selects one sentence from the response and we go around the room reading our lines, confirming that every reaction is honored. I review each written response and write each student a brief note but I do not grade the responses as these are exercises and warm ups. (Students later can select these items for evaluation and place them in their grading folder and writing notebook.)

Photography

Many students are visual learners who see before they write. Photography offers them a myriad of opportunities to develop topics and details. Not all writers need this impetus to writing, and I am selective about overusing any precomposing or collecting activity. But for students that need doors of awareness opened for them, photos can help.

Take a good collection of photos from the library, the media center, or your own collection. For instance, use the powerful Depression photos taken by Dorothea Lange, Ben Shahn, Walker Evans, or the dramatic collection of Civil War photos taken by Matthew Brady, Edward O'Sullivan, and Alexander Gardner. Gardner and O'Sullivan also captured some of our first views of the West and its people.

Start with one photo or a slide. What do you see? What is happening? Who are these people? Look at the angles, the focus, and the textures. Why did the photographer take this picture? What happened just before this shot? Right after it happened?

Photographers talk about being *in the zone,* so engrossed in their subject they snap naturally as they anticipate the scene and lose themselves in the world of their camera eye. How does this translate to writing? Like good writing, good photos have order, tension, simplicity, and dynamics. Freeman Patterson (1979) talks of "thinking sideways," which involves chance and encouraging new ways of looking at things. To think sideways, we have to move all around a subject.

In photography you learn to switch lenses to see different views of the same thing—wide angle, portrait, telephoto. Writers need to see the forests and the trees, the leaves and sky. By looking sideways, writers can build up a mass of information about their subject. In the same way that most of an iceberg is underwater and unseen, we should know more about our subject than is ever shown in one paper. The best classes for photography connections are those in which student artists share through writing what they try to do with cameras or oils or watercolors.

CLINICS AND MINILESSONS

At a tennis match I was photographing, Billie Jean King fired the racquet after a missed shot. I picked up the racquet and handed it to her. On the racquet handle was imprinted, "Keep your eyes on the ball. Keep your head down." I figured if a nine-time Wimbledon champ could use reminders, so could an English teacher.

In my teaching notebook, I maintain a list of possible clinics. This allows me a personal scorecard of things I do each year and possible responses to reading and evaluating the students' finished products. I find clinics valuable because they are quick, concentrated, and have the opportunity for students to put the ideas into practice immediately.

Early in the year, I give a clinic on what I consider to be *good* writing. This allows students to hear me talk about writing, while giving them baseline data about the class. Some people would like one standard of perfect writing, but there isn't one. Writing varies according to personal preference, though I believe we can agree on some conditions present within all good writing.

My first ingredient is interest. Is the piece interesting to read? This is subjective and changes as we change and develop our reading habits. I never used to read nature books and thought they were boring. Now I love them. So what happened? Did the books get better or did my understanding of the quality within the books change? Probably a bit of both. You may prefer Rachel Carson and Lewis Thomas while I prefer Sally Carrighar, Sue Hubbell, and Annie Dillard. They are all superior writers who illustrate *interesting* as an active writing verb.

Other ingredients in my recipe for good writing include images that make ideas clear, words I wish I had used, words whose sound makes poetry out of prose, a variety of strong sentences, and an ending I wish was a new beginning.

Clinics I often find myself conducting on general classroom management include:

How to listen in a group.
How to listen to a partner.
How to share in a group.
How to share with a partner.
How to ask questions (an ongoing clinic).
What you do when finished writing.

Specific clinics on writing include:

What do writers do?
How to find topics (another ongoing clinic).
How to locate and collect topics.
How to approach writing.
How to collect details.
How to plan an approach to a paper.
How to find information.
How to draft.
What to do when stuck.
How to conference with yourself.
How to improve titles.
How to improve leads.
How to edit.
How to peer edit.
How to proofread.
How to publish.
What is style in writing?

What is focus?
How and when to end.
How to add and/or reorder information.
How to use free writing for a structured piece.
How to revise.
How to write for other classes.
How to make an ordinary subject speak.

Early clinics will center on more basic strategies and vary depending on the students' background in process writing. Many of these topics overlap. Note that I never use them in this order, nor do I use all of these every year.

A Sample Clinic on Collecting

Collecting is one clinic I sometimes introduce. What students collect is part of many warm-up lists I ask them to compile. Why do we collect? I collect photos for writing ideas and techniques. I learned how to take tennis pictures from studying how the pros captured action. I collect pencils. Any I see laying around school I pick up, clean, sharpen, and put in the pencil bin. No one in my class will ever not write because they don't have a pencil. I collect student writing samples. I collect words I like to say out loud: *cellar door, pomegranate, Capiabianco, wisenheimer, ratatouille, couscous, zydeco.* I show them my reporter's notebooks filled with words, phrases, and lines that I will use one day. I collect writing ideas and show them folders filled with bits and pieces of things I will write about one day: musical generation gaps, the Amish and the Hutterites, stones in Ireland, growing up, looking for olives in Spanish bistros. I collect professional writing samples of good lines and quotes. I also collect sea glass and book marks, egg cups and trading cards.

What do you collect, I ask them? Any card collectors? I ask this positively as if they all collect because I want them to think about what they have and what is important to them. And if they don't collect, I want them to want to start.

I want them to hear and understand long-term interests. I want them to care, learn, follow, and delve deeply into at least one subject. To follow through is an important learning step. What would you like to collect if you had the wherewithal? Why do people collect weird things like old license plates, Elvis pillows, hubcaps, spoons, or Gene Autry gear?

TALKING BACK

When we read out loud, our words talk back to us, the mind generates more ideas and avenues to explore. Some students ignore these thoughts and try to just recopy. Model talking back in a think-aloud using the overhead. Reread a piece to go forward and talk out loud as your mind offers you other ideas. Sometimes a better topic will evolve. Let the student know that it is OK to change topics, but tell them not to throw away any drafts. What looks like trash today may be a golden idea tomorrow.

READING ALOUD

Students seldom get real feedback in schools. In writing class, students need constant and ongoing feedback, evaluation, and information. Students get nervous about reading aloud. Yet it is an important and valid element in writing process classrooms. How do we establish this routine?

Early in the year I develop *go-rounds*. I try to put students at ease and let them know from day one that we will be sharing. I establish a routine and the attitude that all of us in here are hard-working writers who deserve respect. This breaks the barrier some students have of not speaking out in class and forever holding their voice in check.

My students share both finished and unfinished pieces. With the latter, students may be stuck, not sure if they have enough information, or don't know how to end. So they read the paper to elicit responses, questions, and comments.

Some classes need constant clinics on being helpful and not critical. Like some teachers, some students take the easy way out and do nothing but find mistakes. There is only one teacher in the room, I tell them. And I took the college course on being the teacher. They are to be the listeners. As the students offer responses, I have someone take notes and hand them to the writer so she can now work independently at her desk. For those students who hesitate to read in front of the entire class, I arrange a small-group reading with other students that seem to be receptive but use the same routine: the writer states the problem(s) and then the listeners take notes.

It is important for beginning writers to understand that the questions, comments, and suggestions are not absolute. The readers could misinterpret or not know enough to be helpful, so the writer has to consider each comment separately. They are only suggestions that can be discarded. (The notes, however, are kept as part of the whole process package and become part of the folder.)

THE IMPORTANCE OF SHARING

Reading aloud certainly helps for dialogue, poems, and plays, but it is just as relevant for all writers. To hear our words read by ourselves or someone else can demonstrate bumpy areas of need and smooth areas of success. What we can *see* by hearing is an important part of the composing process.

Writers need to hear words in action. We write for real audiences, a community of writers who listen and enjoy as well as suggest. Sharing shows off work in another type of "publishing." We let developing writers know we enjoy the reading by authors in this room. Writers in the class can explain how a problem was solved or discovered and we all learn from this talk about the writer's process.

Some teachers use one day as a reading or sharing day. I like to spread it around and have readings when they are needed. No matter how involved students are, a full class of listening is difficult. I don't think we can appreciate hearing so many at one time, and I want every reading to be an active lifeline. Spontaneous readings when a student is stuck or successful is a more viable teaching and learning time than a whole class set at the same pace.

Model by celebrating writers and writing. Stop the class to read something a student wrote that is special or surprising or intriguing. Let them know you can't wait to hear more. Ask about a solution to yesterday's problem. And always be honest; teenagers have a built-in crud detector.

READING THE PROS

Beginning writers need to hear words charged and exploding with meaning. As a teacher I believe it is my responsibility to provide this by reading everyday or at least several times a week. I have read at the beginning of classes and I have read the last five minutes of class. Neither is better. But we need to let students hear words in action, well spoken, and appreciated for their impact, power, and beauty. I may not tell them all this as it could be too much for students to handle. My math teacher friend James Crawford, however, tells his calculus students that math is love, truth, and beauty!

I also make sure I read good writing from a variety of sources: clothing catalogs, newspapers, sports magazines, ads, student writing, posters, picture books, nature articles, and comic strips. I fill a folder with sample readings and constantly collect new ones, sorting them as the year goes on. I encourage students to bring in examples as well.

PEER EDITING AND PROOFING

My community of writers helps each other. I start with small groups of students who seem to be friendly and then pair up students and lead the first conference discussions. Other students become interested in what we are doing and want to try too. Soon there are several groups around the room.

Yet some classes never reach that stage of wanting to peer edit. Often these classes are competitive to the point of being unwilling to help each other or they have strong cliques. Some classes take longer to assimilate; once I worked all year and never got a group to be collaborators. But I work hard to overcome this problem because students have a right to peer feedback. Fortunately, you can still achieve a lot in classes without peer conferences.

If we plan to develop peer tutors, we need to work on our ability to monitor groups through observation and participation. We have to set the tone and show them that revision counts. Let students tell us what works. As they get comfortable with tutoring, evaluate groups by asking what happened and why some things didn't work. At the same time use revision questions in whole-class workshops with professional and student drafts. Students become more comfortable with peer editing repeating once they've internalized the lead questions. See Peter Elbow (1973) for more details.

It is also important to teach students how to be peer readers. Students should not write each other's papers but be concerned and responsive listeners. I let students request a peer reader early in a draft, in the middle of writing, or after self-editing. I use a chart to show students what their roles are as writer and as peer reader.

Writer	*Peer Reader*
Reads the piece aloud.	Listens and takes notes.
	Summarizes what they heard the paper say.
Listens.	Points to good features.

| Questions the listener. | Questions the writer for more information about unclear sections. Answers the writer. |

WORKSHOPPING A PAPER

Workshopping a paper in front of the whole class is an excellent teaching device. I like to workshop a draft from which a student has specific questions to ask the audience, perhaps regarding a title, the lead, or information. It could also be an average paper we want the class to help improve. (I always ask permission, in private, before doing this so if the student doesn't want his name used few will know the author.) We may look at a paper that received a good grade but still could be improved with tighter revision. Since one or two papers selected to receive grades must be revised papers, and final exams include a revised paper, most students are happy for the feedback. The class talks about places and ways to improve and offers many suggestions. But I tell the writer to listen with discretion and select only those suggestions she thinks will improve the paper.

CONFERENCING WITH STUDENTS

Teachers in a process workshop room must be observant, know what's going on, and learn what's working and what else is needed. Because students work on their own or in teams, our authority isn't eliminated. In truth we have more responsibility. We need to see and know everything that is going on in the room, even if it is only a subtle understanding. Don't abdicate your role as teacher. Be alert to strengths and possibilities within a team. When conferencing, offer more than one suggestion, but don't write the paper by suggesting too much. Writers not only need choices and freedom, they need limits and discipline. Free choice is not a license for recklessness.

There are no magic questions, but there are some key questions to repeat. Repeat these so students adopt them as their own: "What are you working on?" "How's it going?" "What are you doing next?" "Tell me more." "I'll be interested to read more and see what you decide to do." I try to focus on large issues, not on a missing comma or misspelling. Sometimes a typed or printed version helps so handwriting won't get in the way of meaning.

As teachers we need writing principles in mind when we work with writers in order to have a sense of effective language to communicate.

My writing principles include having high interest levels, solid and clear information, a balance of anecdotes and facts, a definable attitude, a sense of details, strong nouns and verbs, a succinct focus, connections to life beyond the paper, a sense of verbal style, and a careful and thoughtful presentation.

What Does a Process Writing Classroom Look Like?

After they begin, most student writers will move to differing stages within the writing process. At first many students will just be putting pen or pencil to paper, but this alone is not writing. As the days, weeks, and months go on, the students in one class may be doing such varied acts as jotting notes, doodling, trying endings, editing, or conferencing with peers. Learning to go about writing through a palette of activities is a sign of a student's development and progress. Make note of their activities so you can later use this information; evaluate the student writer on these elements within the process rather than only on a final product.

Response Teaching

Murray (1985) refers to conferences as "response teaching": the teacher responds to the work-in-progress of a developing writer. We don't have to know everything about the piece to respond. We only have to be an animated listener and, based on our reading experience, try to see the becoming writer as a maker of meaning. Conferences are short and frequent talks with student writers based on the belief that all students have the potential to write something worth reading given time and productive feedback.

We have to be prepared for conference teaching—it's exhausting. Unlike lectures that keep us in total control, we have no idea what the next student will ask or need. So we must be quick of mind and make use of our knowledge, insights, and experiences, not to mention balancing the hundreds of things that go on while one writes.

Conferences in our rooms do call for changes such as restructuring the room for movement and group work and setting up an environment of involvement. Eliminate lectures on writing, but provide time for work with individual students or pairs rather than with the whole class

Through conferences, teachers act as catalysts so students accomplish better writing. Conferences happen during the writing process when most writers need the help. They can happen at any time during the process and in any place, even the corridor. The purpose is to assist writers in focusing on their writing.

Conferences could include conversation between

teacher and student
student and student
student in a reflective self-conference
student and the small group
teacher and the whole class.

Our role is to get the students to move along though the stages of the writing process. To this end, we ask open-ended questions. The main point of any conference is for the listener to hear and then respond in a caring manner without taking ownership of the piece.

In a teacher-student conference, start by asking where she is in the process. From that answer, the next steps fall into place (sort of). Have the student read a problem section while you listen. This way you can focus on the content (meaning, interest, details, focus, and logic) and ignore first-draft errors in mechanics. If you read an early draft without the student present, don't hold a pen or pencil. (The English teacher's twitch can overcome us—mark that error! slash that mistake!)

Talks or conferences are ongoing, so set no specific time for editing or topic-search conferences. Once students get writing, they are all over the process map, thus our talk with them will also follow no clear map. One student will still be looking for a topic while others need content assistance.

Talking about searching for a topic centers on helping students select and narrow topics for writing; such talk happens anytime and all the time. Our role is to be alert to new topics students are interested in. Talk about a developing paper happens as a discovery draft is finished or when a student is stuck. Here again, we need to listen, point out what we like, and ask questions that could lead to more information in the piece. "Could you explain that more?" "What do you mean by that?" "Can you give me some examples?" "What's the most important thing here?" "Why did you pick this subject?" Ask questions that can get the student to focus: "Tell me again what happened—without looking at your draft."

Revising talk usually occurs after a draft is completed, and editing conferences happen after a piece is finished but before publishing. I try to direct students to check their skills list so they can review the editing on previous papers and then reinforce those previous editing strengths. I try not to take a paper in hand but prefer to have the students read sections to me. Then I cannot see mistakes and I listen for possibilities. After a piece has been selected, revised, and edited, we may talk about publishing. I ask why the student selected this piece to be published. If needed, I remind the student about form, mechanics, and presentation.

I want to make students aware of their own process of writing and the overall processes of writing different genres, so I look forward to talking about their process in composing a piece. Here is where the real learning about writing happens. When we talk about our own process we internalize more to recall later. This metacognition happens anytime, certainly after a paper is "finished."

For the papers that are graded to meet school requirements, I talk with each student writer. I want students to hear me discuss their growth as a writer. While our talk has been preceded by a note on the paper, now they can question, react, and hear my tone of voice face to face. If they have no questions, then I ask, "What is the hardest part of writing for you?" "The easiest part?" "What do you plan to work on next?"

PROOFREADING CHECKLISTS

With some students, I need to make a specific checklist of items to double-check. I tell them that most writers have similar checklists, though the list is often in the head of professional writers. For beginning writers, it helps to see the list, and we keep it in the folder as a reminder of things to polish in any paper. What follows is an sample checklist from one developing class:

Each sentence begins with a capital letter.
The letter *I* is always capitalized when it forms a word by itself.
Each sentence ends with some form of punctuation.
The names of people and important places are capitalized.
Speech marks *(" ")* are used around conversations.
Each new paragraph is indented.
Spelling is checked and corrected to the best of the writer's ability.
The writer's handwriting is clear and legible.

There is also a place to add other areas of focus for individual students. Even so, you may say they should already know all these rules.

But remember, writing is not an easy-to-accomplish task, and a tangible checklist can remind some students of things they already know. Quality control is nothing to be ashamed of.

HOW DO YOU LEAD STUDENTS TO WRITE IN DIFFERENT GENRES?

I developed a set of folders that focus on different genres. I began this routine with a class that loved to collect, categorize, and give order to things. All of the students selected one or more genres to read, analyze, and select samples for the folders. Then they wrote introductions for each folder and directions on writing in that genre. Their information was reviewed by other students and placed in separate folders. They also published an annotated index of these folders identifying the authors. The subject of the folders included ads, anecdotes, autobiography, book reviews, character sketches, classification, columns, commentaries, comparison/contrast, definition(both short and extended), descriptions, directions (both factual and creative), essay exams, fantasy, interviews, journals, leads, personal letters, business letters, lists, mysteries, myths, outlining, notetaking, personality profiles, *New Yorker* profiles, poetry, quotations (both using and writing), reporting news, reporting sports, science fiction, student newspapers from around New England, resumes, reviews, roots, sentence combining, short stories, songs (both how to write them and how to use them for writing ideas), spelling aids, sports features, study skills, style, summaries, travel, vocabulary, word banks, patterns, textures, sounds, smells, visual qualities, and writers on writing.

Though I started out assigning the same genre to every student at the same time, now I am interested in letting students choose to write in a variety of genres. This includes free choice multigenre reports and theme study, which often capture the imagination of curious students.

HOW DO YOU MANAGE ALL THESE ACTIVITIES?

Students usually want consistency and accept changes better within a routine they understand. Writing is difficult enough, so the discipline within a classroom should be predictable, not harsh. Here are some guidelines I set:

- Write on one side of a page only.
- Date every page. "Date the page every time you come back to it," I tell students; some pages end up with three or four dates. This tells me about the student's process.
- Save everything.
- Initial all pages. Where the name and heading goes on drafts is not that important as long as the name is on the first page. I recommend initialing the rest of the pages.
- Use crossouts, not erasures. Erasing takes too much time and makes a mess. And what we erase today in a fit of displeasure, may tomorrow be exactly what is needed to complete an award-winning piece.
- Use your time wisely.
- Do not interfere with other students' processes. Writing is too hard to be interrupted by others.
- Learn by hearing. This seems like a strange rule but it is important in a workshop environment to learn the importance of talk. They need to listen to questions and answers.
- Conference on the perimeter of the room. Don't disturb others.
- Know how to operate in the room. This includes when to use the writing table, how to get folders, where materials are stored, how to share, what to do when finished, how to read your own paper, and general classroom management.

These rules are really operating procedures. I do not introduce them all at one time, especially to a younger group or to students who seem to have little background in writing. I scatter them in the first few weeks as relevant issues come up in class rather than reciting all of them at once on day one.

I know some teachers prefer to type all the rules on sheets of paper to hand out that first week but that doesn't work for me. I find students remember them longer when a brief oral or dramatic statement is made. Also, I don't make rules if they are not needed. Thus, the same rules are not appropriate for all classes.

When a rule does seem relevant, I introduce it in a short workshop lesson. For instance, one day I will show the classes a box or file stand. "This is the editing box. After you have worked a piece through and have had two students edit your paper but before you publish it, you can use me as an editor. This is not an early draft—which I'll look at with you in class. When you are almost finished and if you want me as an editor, leave your paper here and I'll look it

over by class the next day." This technique also reviews other working concepts within the class.

WHY IS MODELING IMPORTANT?

Modeling is a form of teaching. Craftspeople, for instance, always
talk about their tools; artists learn early the importance of choosing
the correct paint tools. Teachers should show interest in our tools. I
tell students about how my choice of pen depends on my moods: a
thin point for those sharp, on-edge days; thick, bold points for gray
and dull days; cheap pens with clicks for nervous days; and smooth,
expensive gift pens for signature days. Color varies as well. Pens are
my tools.

What does this have to do with teaching English? I believe it helps
students see I'm serious about writing. I might ask if they have a
favorite pen or pencil. Over the next several days I will hear a lot of
stories about pens and pencils and be given a lot of them.

Students do not see teachers write enough. They see us talking,
reading, viewing, reprimanding, ordering, conferencing, and sometimes listening. They need to see us writing. Show them on an overhead how you insert information using carets, and how you read
what you wrote yesterday to get going today. Model whatever they
need to move along the road to better writing.

By such modeling we build a community of writers. Be serious and
positive about writing. Show them to trust and respect each other's
reactions and thoughts. Accept and enjoy and learn from the variety
within the class.

HOW IMPORTANT IS CHOICE?

Balance free choice with assigned topics. Students should find their
own topics and write about what they know, but in school and in life
they will also be called upon to write on given subjects. Help students find their own angle and use their writing processes with
assigned papers. Provide time to discuss assignments from your own
and other classes.

Assigning the same topic for every student closes down student
options. Students have not had the same experiences and need to
select their own topics, but as teachers we may also need to show them
possibilities within their own experiences. How many times since college have you had to write an analysis of Elizabethan sonnets? Your

college papers may be brilliant, but hold off sharing them with four-teen year olds. As you plan each assignment, ask yourself if it advances their learning. Then test your answer by first doing the assignment. With this as a foundation, you can better judge the value of the assignment.

WHY IS SELF-EVALUATION IMPORTANT TO WRITING?

I want students to evaluate their own writing and writing process. Introspection is another important aspect of learning and under-standing, one with long-ranging implications. To achieve this inner look, I have students write about their process. At first I might just note one or two questions: What is the best part of this paper? What did you learn about yourself as a writer? For a review, I ask them questions on a longer sheet. I gradually move up to more sophisti-cated analysis using writing process notebooks in which I ask stu-dents to carry on a dialogue: What were you trying to do? What writ-ing techniques worked? What didn't? What are you going to try next time? What unanswered questions do you have?

And always I ask students to tell me what else I need to know as I read their papers. Often these process evaluations are more informa-tive about the writer's process than the papers. As the students become more sophisticated, I then ask them to analyze their own writing through marginal notes (Kearns 1991).

READING WITH A WRITER'S EYE

If the students do not seem to have a knack for writing interesting pieces, I might do a whole class clinic on reading with a writer's eye. Using either a good student example or an article that mirrors what they are writing—such as an expository piece—we would look closely at what that writer did to make us interested. Typical issues to con-sider include:

Where did your interest pick up? Find that section. Look at the author's words, arrangement, and punctuation. What did she do to get your attention?

What character did you really like or identify with? Reread sections with that character. What did the author do with his words to help you see or know that character?

Read sections you particularly like aloud. Get close to the rhythm of the words. Read aloud some of your own words.
What general strategies did the author use?

Reading with a writer's eye means seeing what writers do with words. I suggest students mark words and lines they like and ask themselves if they could try something like that. What ideas does the reading give you? How does it extend your thinking, challenge what you believe, or connect with what you know? Next, we go right to our drafts and write with a reader's eye. For instance, listen to what Diane Ackerman does with vanilla: "Saturate your nose with glistening, soulful vanilla and you can *taste* it. It's not like walking through a sweetshop, but more subterranean and wild" (1993). I also use interesting lines from student papers as examples of writing with a reader's eye:

> There will be little rain this spring. No April showers. No May flowers. The temperatures will be unseasonably high and the friendly cardinal won't be singing on your windowsill.

> "Yes, John. You have set back academic progress another few years, just like a baby who gets the candy. You'll still get your rimhangers, three-point shooters and quick point-guards while you keep shakin' that rattle, suckin' that thumb, and throwin' those tantrums!"

WHO ARE WRITERS?

I tell the students all the stories I know about how writers work. Even stories about people they may not consider writers can be helpful. Jazz performer Pat Metheny keeps a journal of concert tours to detail each show to study his performing routines. Baseball player Andre Dawson keeps a journal to understand the tendencies of each pitcher he faces. I tell them about a young lawyer in Mississippi who took notes on courtroom interactions then used these jottings as the foundations for his best-selling novels. His name: John Grisham.

As teachers, we should have knowledge of writers as writers: John McPhee, Hemingway, and Yeats. We should know that E. B. White wrote hundreds of questions he had about spiders and trumpeter swans and then got answers by reading, talking with, and writing to experts. Some of this information was used in his children's stories and the rest became "background." We need to have such anecdotes about writers. For instance, Colleen McCullough was very upset at an editor who removed a comma from the first paragraph. She said it was an important comma! Eudora Welty used sewing pins to tie together pieces of her writing so she could visually rearrange her stories. John McPhee has an office where he goes everyday to write because that's his "job." Many writers and teachers know Hemingway rewrote *A Farewell to Arms* thirty-nine times, but few have heard his reason for all these rewrites: he said he wanted to "get the words right." That's what all writers are trying to do.

Reading about characters who are writers can also open doors of insight about how authors work. I maintain a list of books whose characters are writers, such as:

Avi, *True Confessions of Charlotte Doyle*
Anne Fine, *The Book of the Banshee*
Paul Fleischman, *Bull Run*
James Forman, *Becca's Story*
Karen Hesse, *Letters from Rifka*
Kathryn Lasky, *Pageant*
Mary Lyons, *Letters from a Slave Girl*
Gary Paulsen, *Woodsong*
Gary Soto, *Fire in My Hands*
Diary of Latoya Hunter: My First Year in Junior High

Books about writers and the memoirs and autobiographies of writers include:

Clyde Robert Bulla, *A Grain of Wheat*
Beverly Cleary, *Girl from Yamhill*
Pat Cummings, *Talking with Artists* and *Speaking for Ourselves: Autobiographical Sketches of Young Authors*
Roald Dahl, *Boy: Tales of Childhood*
Jean Fritz, *Homesick*
Don Gallo, *Authors' Insights: Turning Teenagers into Readers and Writers*
Eloise Greenfield, *Childtimes*
Trina Schart Hyman, *Self-Portrait*
Jean Little, *Little by Little* and *Stars Come Out Within*
Pamela Lloyd, *How Writers Write*
Milton Meltzer, *Starting from Home: A Writer's Beginning*
Farley Mowat, *Born Naked*

Phyllis Reynolds Naylor, *How I Came to Be a Writer*
Eudora Welty, *One Writer's Beginnings*

HELPING STUDENTS REVISE

Teachers complain that students don't revise. I've found students don't revise because they do not know how to revise, much less proofread or edit. Though some editing, revising and proofing go on during the writing process, every writer needs time to reread drafts, make changes, and check for errors in mechanics and usage. If we do not give students time to revise, then we should not mark their work down for these mistakes. And if we do not show them how to revise and proofread, how will they ever know?

They first have to have something to revise. But they do not revise every piece they write; the work of revision should begin after they collect a folder filled with possibilities (of course, some revising occurs as we write). Then they select the one paper they want to publish. This is the time to teach them how to revise. Some students begin with just mechanical, spelling, and small content changes before they mature enough to revise for meaning and organization. By senior high I expect writers to be able to revise for emphasis, clarity, and audience. But at any age or developmental stage, you will find writers who naturally revise for style—rhythm, tone, texture, and surprises. Revision is hard work, but it is at the heart of good writing. As their mentor and model, you may need to

- Give students time to correct their own mistakes.
- Teach them to proofread their own papers.
- Use minilessons or clinics to show how to be an editor and a proofreader.
- Use the computer to print out their papers, which makes errors easier to spot.
- Conference with students around the room as they are writing. Read for content first, and then edit with them as they get ready for publishing.

One element of revising is improving the order of information to achieve the greatest reader impact. Here is a great place to use the writing notes of E. B. White (Neumeyer 1982). Students know White from *Charlotte's Web, Stuart Little,* and *Trumpet of the Swans.* In his notes you can see and hear his struggle. Though not primarily a children's writer, White worked at his craft once he decided to try children's literature.

Frequently students need help on how to reorder to achieve the strongest order, and reordering requires revising. Remember, many developing writers confuse revision with recopying, which represents dull, tedious, and unproductive work. There are many tangible, active, and even fun ways to reorder and revise. I teach them to reorder information by using

carets to insert details
arrows to move sentences or paragraphs
letters or numbers keyed to a separate sheet for easier additions
cutting and pasting instead of recopying
writing only on one side of a page so you can cut and move
wide margins where you can add more details
skipping lines so you can easily insert information
crossouts instead of erasures to make writing less messy and more clear
transposing lines to reposition letters and words
pens of different colors to distinguish different readings.

Making mistakes is not embarrassing; letting the errors go is embarrassing. All writers need editors, but writers are usually their own worst editors; we see what we wanted to say, not what we actually wrote. Writers are not always good editors, and I know excellent editors who are not good writers.

Establish an atmosphere in which polishing is expected. In every class, time is needed to right the writing. Following the conventions of American language is a necessity—the student's responsibility. It is the teacher's responsibility to make sure they know how, but it is not our responsibility to revise for them. Our editing is not writing.

I set aside a table as the editing center. I decorate it with the tools of revising and editing: peace and quiet, dictionaries, scissors, tape, and style and usage books.

In some classes, every student becomes an editor, focusing on margins, handwriting, leads, endings, titles, periods, semicolons, commas and so on. Two or three students are usually the editors for spelling, a couple for run-on sentences, maybe two for topic development. We all get involved, and in those classes in which we take our roles seriously—even in the midst of laughter—the electricity ignites a glow of writing excitement that is difficult to explain. The students each select one piece to revise and edit and then begin looking for student editors. The whole room turns into a workplace, with no one at the front of the room. One day my principal came to observe me but said she'd be back when I was *teaching*. Before she could leave, one student asked her to listen to a paper and the principal became just one more class editor.

After the papers go through two editors, students can ask for my reading by putting the paper in my editing box. They can write specific questions on attached sheets about form, usage, mechanics, and so on. I reply overnight (rather like a good truth fairy!).

LEARNING BY OVERHEARING

As I talk with one student about editing or revising or proofreading, other students hear and connect the information to something they wondered about. Peer editing works the same way in some classes, but flies like a brick house in others. Grade competition can work against cooperation.

Students who conference and read each other's papers also learn about their own papers. By teaching others, they teach themselves how to revise and edit and create stronger papers. Soon they will read their own drafts more critically. Murray (1978) reminds us that the "student in the writing course must develop the ability to evaluate his own accomplishment, to spot his own problems, and to correct them."

TOPIC DEVELOPMENT THROUGH CONTACT SHEETS

Poor topic development is a problem all writers have. Helping students understand topic development and then implement their understanding is difficult. No one approach solves the issue for every student, so I carry around a folder full of ideas.

When students come to class with no experience in developing longer pieces of writing, I have used contact sheets. These are sheets of pictures the size of the negative that show all prints on a roll at once. With magnifying glasses, we look at several samples to see the variety and depth of the topic the photographer captured. I found oversized contact sheets in photo magazines and as posters available from film companies. I even bring in my own sheets on lobstering, tennis, old barns, babies, and school teams. Students search for the strongest picture to be the lead in a photo essay. After deciding, they explain their choice to a partner, who also examines the sheet. Then they exchange roles so each takes a turn defending that choice. By trying to select one out of many, they usually end up reviewing and discussing the quality of all the pictures. And like so many aspects of writing and photography, there are no wrong answers, just pictures and words that work better.

Next we talk about developing our own contact sheets. First, students select a subject within their reach, say a younger brother or sister, pet, friend, or sport. I recommend that they take outdoor photos as built-in flashes are unreliable and unpredictable. After selecting a subject, we take a topic no one has chosen and brainstorm the variety of shots possible. With skiing, our list might include putting skis in a car, carrying them to the hut, putting skis on, riding the lift, reaching the top of the trail, coming down, falling, eating lunch, seeing racks of skis, talking with friends, and noting the colors of ski outfits.

The goal is to see details in a single subject and to develop unity and visualize interest. Students have examined doors, signs, rainy days, houses, trucks, textures, clouds, light and dark patterns, squares, hats, and stores. Students then develop their storyboard of potential ideas. Usually I give a tight deadline for this activity to avoid losing the goal. I let them have two weeks including three weekends. A local camera store offered development at a reduced price for us and loaned several basic cameras for students without one at home.

Students are excited to see their own and others' contact sheets. Now I remind them of the purpose: How does this focus translate into writing? The success or failure of the exercise is determined by how clearly they see this activity relating to their writing.

CAN WE TEACH STYLE?

I don't know if anyone can teach how to write with style or how to develop individual style. Murray (1995b) says style is something you buy at a store. Instead, he writes that "voice is the music that communicates and supports the meaning of what you write. . . . It is voice, more than any other element, that marks excellent writing."

Perhaps his voice is my style, but I know there are certain styles of writing I like and some I do not. I try to help students discover who they like to read and then they figure out what that writer did with words. We can begin to develop a personal style by imitating someone else's.

Style is hard to define but we know it when we see it: Keith Lockhart conducting, John Hancock signing, Boris Becker charging the net. Style is usually defined as a distinctive way of writing, including word choice, phrasing, sentence structure and variety, rhythm, and voice. Style can come with practice. Style involves selection and arrangement, an awareness of words, and an understanding of repetition.

Writers work hard to develop style. Consider this sentence delivered by Ted Kennedy:

"When he left us at forty-six, Jack Kennedy shared that quality of universality. He could talk with a poet or a prime minister, start an astronaut toward the moon, reach a child in the South, throw a spiral pass, haul a sail, write a book, and make a Russian blink."

Here students can see a list with commas in a series and strong verbs. To help students see the language at work, I would type the example in this manner:

> When he left us at 46,
> Jack Kennedy shared that quality of universality.
> He could
> talk with a poet or a prime minister,
> start an astronaut toward the moon,
> reach a child in the South,
> throw a spiral pass,
> haul a sail,
> write a book, and
> make a Russian blink.

Students can visually understand the balance and the parallelism, the structure and variety.

DYNAMIC SYMMETRY

For whatever reason, students tend to employ even-numbered compound structures. In actual use, uneven combinations such as three, five, seven, or nine are more pleasant to our ears. The rule of dynamic symmetry—the theory that unequal distributions are better—has been around since the sixth century BC. Many creative people profess this sensibility, including painters, landscape designers, and architects.

In music, for instance, there are tricolons—a series of three—the offbeat. In graphic design there is the rule of threes. I teach students to find three verbs, phrases, or adjectives that describe the action. Patterns of three break the rhythm while advancing the action. In her *Summer of My German Soldier,* Bette Greene illustrates her story with sharp tricolons to accentuate her style: "The train braked, screeched, and finally came to a halt": "The aroma of coffee perking, griddle cakes rising, and bacon frying . . .".; "A car passed. Chrome hubcaps mirrored the sun's rays. I began collecting those gray white stones that were within lazy reach. Improve your aim. Hit the hubcap. Win a prize." Once students recognize these lyrical arrangements, they can practice writing with rhythm and style.

In his book *Inner Tennis* Tim Gallwey (1976) calls for keeping the game simple and natural. The goal in tennis is to hit the ball over the net one more time. Players know the rules, but they don't hold them consciously in mind when playing. Practice allows tennis to be natural, as it does with writing (and teaching).

HOW DO STUDENTS ACHIEVE GOOD WRITING?

I have asked my students about how they reach their best writing:

I write about things that touch me, like a flower, some friends, or a special day. . . . I open up my heart and let what I feel come alive. . . . I flick on a switch in my head and write about something I feel strongly about.

I use the split-sheet method. It gives me a chance to brainstorm and push my thoughts so that I squeeze out every bit of information. It gives me an idea if more is needed as well as a hint of order to incorporate these facts.

Teachers should tell students not to be inhibited about what they write. If they have strong feelings about something, they should let it out. Here's where the best writing is done, when the thoughts are genuine.

There are very few authors who write about something they have no interest in. If teachers would let their students write about what they wanted to, nine times out of ten I think they would see greater results and more imagination.

WHAT ELSE DOES A TEACHER DO TO ENHANCE WRITING INSTRUCTION?

Develop a writers' vocabulary: *cut and paste, graph* for *paragraph, draft, lead, publish, polish, edit, proof,* and with computers *fonts, margins,* and *delete.*

Let them talk about their process. Ask, "How did you go about writing this paper? It is your best one so far. How did you get that idea or find that title?" Share students' process of composing with the class by posting the various stages of development on the bulletin board.

Be alert to student problems and questions. How does each student approach the writing? How does each student make use of time? How does each student engage in the process of composing?

Listen to student talk before school, during lunch, before class, and in study hall, then make their out-of-class experiences and knowledge relevant to writing. This also gives you ideas to suggest for writing topics. Learning isn't confined by the ringing of bells or dates on a calendar; learning is a never-ending Möbius strip.

WRITING STRATEGIES

Over the years, I developed an inventory of solutions, options, and strategies for writers to use when they have problems. Most are on the tip of my tongue, but I keep a list in my three-ring binder that I add to every few months. It also serves as a reference point when I prepare to conference with student writers.

Process Problems

Don't Know How to Get Started

Talk out your ideas with a partner who will take notes and ask questions. Use those notes and questions to start.

Skip the first paragraph and work on the rest of the paper.

Read a paper on a topic that interests you. How did that author start?

Reread an article with a lead that made an impression on you. Imitate that lead; you can always change it later.

Put your name, the date, the weather, and what you plan to do at the top of the page. Then start writing.

Read Annie Lamott's chapter "Shitty First Drafts" in *Bird by Bird* (1994).

Don't Know Where to Go Next?
Start a new paper.
Be a conference partner.
Give your paper to an editor.
Help revise the teacher's paper.
Start or add to your Can Do list, showing skills and writing attributes
    you can do.
Read your Can Do list and make sure you did what you can do.
Add an illustration, map, graph, or drawing.
Add a glossary of terms readers will need.
Write an "about the author" description of yourself in the third
    person.
Go read a friend's paper and conference.

Do You Get Stuck?
Get a partner and conference about your topic.
Consider the five Ws: who, what, when, where, and why. Which are
    needed to help your topic?
Have someone listen to your paper and write down the questions they
    have.

Topic Problems

Are There Too Many Topics in One Paper?
List all topic areas and develop the best one. Focus on one element.
Consider rearranging; get scissors.
Map out or brainstorm one part of your topic.
Cut one topic out, paste it on a blank page, and use it as a beginning
    point for that paper.

Don't Have Any New Topics?
Check your future topic list for ideas.
Look at your brainstorming lists for ideas.
Recheck unfinished compositions at the back of the folder.
Look through a family photo album for stories.
Look in the class albums to see what other students have written about.
Review handouts of past topics lists.

Is Your Paper Too Long and Boring?
Have the guts to cut.
Remove every dull phrase, sentence, and idea.
Try adding a flashback.

Development Problems

Does the Organization Seem Poor?
Rearrange with arrows or scissors.
Start in the middle of your story.
Use the 2–3–1 order for emphasis.

Is the Information Unclear?
Put the paper in your folder and start over on a new angle.
Underline where you think your information is clear; start again at this
   place.
Take a key sentence, put it at the top of a blank page, and add more
   information there.
Include definitions, diagrams, and maps.

Is There Not Enough Information?
Interview someone who has more information on the topic.
Read some basic books on the subject.
Use an insert sheet to add details at a critical section.

Is the Organization Boring?
Point to the best part of the paper and cut the rest.
Rewrite your story to half its size.
Write the piece in one sentence and then develop the important parts.
Try a flashback.
Try starting right in the middle, just before the best or key part.

Detail Problems

Is There a Lack of Detail?
Write a list of details.
Bring in pictures of your subject.
Look at the work of a master writer (e.g., E. B. White).

Does the Title Seem Flat?
List five possible titles ranging from straight to funny.
Find a song with an appropriate phrase.
Borrow a known title that fits and rearrange the words.
Use the most distant title you can find for your paper; make people
   think they missed something.
Look at the last two or three paragraphs. You may have a title there in
   words you have already written.
Look at handouts of titles used by other students for ideas.
Brainstorm fifty titles to strain your brain.

Is There a Lack of Emphasis?
Use the 2–3–1 order of emphasis for sentences, paragraphs, and the whole composition's structure.

Number the most important pieces of information and rearrange to emphasize.

Are the Sentences Too Simple or Similar?
Try combining a few sentences.

Write a sentence with six words or less for emphasis.

Combine related material into a cumulative sentence.

Count the number of words per sentence in a flat paragraph. What patterns do you see?

Are your prepositional phrases at the end of sentences? Try them at the beginning.

How does a rough sentence sound when compared to those around it?

Are There Run-on Sentences?
Read your sentences aloud to yourself. Mark where you need to take a breath and rewrite accordingly.

Read today's newspaper for sentence styles.

Look for sentence and word patterns and then rearrange.

Try a variety of sentence lengths and structures.

Word Choice Problems

Do You Have Weak Word Choices?
Cut the number of adjectives and adverbs.

Cut any cluttering words. Common clutterers include *which, because, there, that,* and *very.*

Read at least one poem.

Look at a photography book for visual help.

Give yourself a dime for every sentence you can reduce by one or two words.

Look at the word bank folder.

Read a section from your favorite author. What does this person do with words?

Read Zinsser's *On Writing Well* for his section on verbs and nouns (1990). His discussion of verbs is the clearest, most active verb piece I have found. Its message clearly directs students, "Active verbs push hard; passive verbs tug fitfully."

Collect verbs that push hard: *strike, soothe, rave, ramble, rant, giggle, snicker, cackle, fry, sear, burn, sizzle, seep, ooze, gush, squash, swagger, screech, clutch, grab, slouch, saunter, amble, trudge, shuffle,* and *glide.*

Describe the walks of Andre Agassi, Sylvester Stallone, Jerry Rice, Cindy Crawford, and Jay Leno without using the word *walk.* Or describe Michael Jordan jumping and dunking without those words (e.g., *springs, floats, swivels, swoops, soars, slams, whumps*).

Describe the sun setting over a city with only "colored" verbs such as *halos, floats, enchants, changes, dazzles, washes, blushes, warms,* and *designs.*

Are You Using Flat or Passive Verbs?

Try writing in the present tense. Read parts of John McPhee's *Levels of the Game,* a wonderful report of a tennis match that will forever be in the *now* with McPhee's use of present tense (1969).

Mechanical Problems

Are There Many Mechanical Errors?

Slow down after you have some ideas on paper.

Do corrections in study hall.

Categorize mistakes to see what types they fall into. Deal with one error pattern at a time.

Research the error and its cause. Refer to resource books such as usage manuals for help.

Fight careless editing.

Take time to proofread.

Check your last paper.

Don't Know How to Improve Your Spelling?

Underline or circle words you are not sure of, but try not to stop while you are composing.

Check your own word list in the folder.

Ask a good speller to circle your mistakes.

Concentrate on your particular spelling problems.

See words within words: *here* is the opposite of *there,* separate *a rat,* and *villain* and *villa.*

Study the *ei* words: *receive, seize, weird, leisure, neither,* and *either.*

Study the *ie* words: *believe, achieve, chief,* and *niece.*

Memorize the words you find difficult to spell.

Invent a temporary spelling until you are ready to publish, then correct the word.

Ask a partner to double-check your words.
See if the word is around the room anyplace. Can you find it in a book you have read?
Use the spellchecker on the computer, if available.

Do You Have Weak Proofreading Skills?
Through workshopping and a clinic, teach students these options:

- Read each line *right to left* to study the spelling of each word more carefully.
- Start at the last sentence and proofread spelling backwards.
- Circle words you know you have to look up.
- Use a blank sheet to cover everything but the line you are proofreading.
- Read quickly for meaning then slowly for errors.
- Use dictionaries, telephone books, atlases, maps, and other references.
- Type the paper onto the computer to see the word printed in black and white.
- Have class editors check spelling.

As teachers we can use notes to ask students about their mistakes: "Do you see all these spelling mistakes? I know you can spell these words. What happened today?" Let the student take responsibility.

WRITING IN A VARIETY OF GENRES

Written communication is the result of seeing an idea clearly and then transferring that picture to words to read as clearly as possible. In photography we may understand how our camera operates and the relation of light to film and the subject. But these are the mechanics of photography, not what makes a snapshot become an artistic statement.

In photography, the moment of truth is when the shutter clicks; capturing the best moment depends on our eye and mind, our experience and anticipation, and sometimes on a risk-taking whim. In writing, there are also moments of truth, times during the composing process when you follow your whim, experience, and knowledge. Like style, whim probably cannot be taught, but we can develop students' experience and knowledge and nurture their whim.

Too often early in my teaching, I found myself assigning types of writing and defining length, date due, and minutiae like the position of the title, but not explaining or exploring what those types of writing really are. What makes this piece a character sketch and not a summary or a story? Each genre has certain ingredients that differentiate it from others. The further a genre moves from personal experience, the harder the genre is initially to achieve and the more the students need time, samples, and ongoing feedback. What follows is a brief overview of some typical genres secondary students write.

Memoirs

Memoirs fill our need to eavesdrop through short, intense glimpses at someone else's life. (Look at the popularity of *People* magazine.) Describing memoirs as ways of inventing the truth, William Zinsser (1987) says, "Unlike autobiography . . . the writer of a memoir takes us back to a corner of his or her life that was unusually vivid or intense—childhood, for instance—or that was framed by unique events. By narrowing the lens, the writer achieves a focus that isn't possible in autobiography; memoir is a window into a life."

Some of today's best writers have written memoirs: Russell Baker, Annie Dillard, Maya Angelou, Bailey White, and Lewis Thomas; there is no shortage of examples.

The key word to consider when selecting the frame of a memoir is *uniqueness*. What was unique about an incident, period, person, or reaction? Students can survey their own timeline to see what could be a possible subject for their memoir. What moment is especially memorable to you? Why? I model searching through my timeline, looking especially at the high and low points in my childhood. I'll never forget the lost feeling when my dog died, my dislike of segregated boy-girl recess, or my fear of an empty house. None of these are big moments, but they are moments full of feeling. And feeling is what we try to capture in memoirs. Not only do students find they can write meaningful memoirs, but they discover a whole new world of reading.

Read aloud the snowball scene from Annie Dillard's *An American Childhood,* a classic example of memoir writing (1987). For more ideas on memoir writing see also *Turning Memories into Memoirs: A Handbook for Writing Lifestories* by Denis Ledoux (1993).

Character and Personality Sketches

Most students need to study a number of character sketches before they are competent enough to write really fine ones. Usually I like to give them this experience with people they have already met (e.g., Atticus Finch, Charles Darnay, Willy Loman, Anne Frank, Scarlet O'Hara). I would add other sketches from writers they may know like this strong example from John McPhee (1971):

> Floyd Elgin Dominy raises beef cattle in the Shenandoah Valley. Observed there, hand on a fence, his eyes surveying his pastures, he does not look particularly Virginian. Of middle height, thickset, somewhat bandy-legged, he appears to have been lifted off a horse with a block and tackle. He wears blue jeans, a white-and-black striped shirt, and leather boots with heels two inches high. His belt buckle is silver and could not be covered with a playing card. He wears a string tie that is secured with a piece of petrified dinosaur bone. On his head is a white Stetson.

McPhee paints Floyd like Andrew Wyeth sketches Christina. In both cases, we have broad lines that suggests details and personality. Both place their people in a time and place in which we can observe them carefully, almost in isolation, yet with a feeling for the action around them. Other authors may not go into so much detail and let the personality evolve with the story. Authors may use one-liners such as we find in Chaucer, or Garson Kanin's *Tracy and Hepburn:* "She's tall, but not as tall as she thinks she is" (1971).

In class we would talk about what Kanin means and what we find out about the actor Katharine Hepburn from this line. Students can imagine what this person may be like. We may play with the phrase: not as smart, fast, old, or whatever else the students offer. Our brainstorming is an important foundation for student writers who may not be able to compile many ideas on their own. Length is not as important in a character sketch as much as an original, clear, and concise view of the person. Take chances, I tell them; sketch with broad strokes; be free and unique in word selection and placement. Some students have a natural feeling for this form of writing, but others may need direction.

Magazine profiles in the *New Yorker* and *Sports Illustrated* may illuminate the format and tone of personality sketches. As you interview, listen for key quotes and attitudes in your writing. Sometimes the structure of the piece evolves as we listen. I tell students to select a focal point such as the person's hands, eyes, stories, words, clothes, voice tones, or passions. They then select details to fill out the picture. Their notes should include physical descriptions, typical actions, likes, dislikes, habits and hobbies, memories, and daily routines. Notes should be filled in immediately after the interview, recording any sense you have for the way your paper will develop. Then mull over what you have.

After getting a handle on this person, consider the organization. A chronological order may not be the logical choice. Such considerations push the personality piece to a higher level of thinking.

I invite students to bring in photographs to help them study their person, but we also look at artists such as Andrew Wyeth, Norman Rockwell, Pablo Picasso, and Henri Matisse. Use the Wyeth print *Albert's Son* to examine facial expressions. What does the expression of mouth show? The eyes? What kind of person is he? What might he say if you were to interrupt him right now? Rockwell's *Saturday Evening Post* covers are also full of stories to explore. See what you have to share.

I suggest students start with their strongest piece of information, leaving the second strongest for the end and use the other details for the middle (a variation on the 2–3–1 rule of emphasis), but each paper should evolve from the material and not from a rule.

Commentaries

Commentaries include editorials, columns, and opinion papers as well as the more common written arguments, persuasive pieces, and position papers. All are meant to make readers understand why the writer thinks the way he does.

Again, practice makes for better writers. Students need to be expressing their opinions, insights, questions, and comments from day one. The more they are given opportunities to stand on their own feet, the better they will be able to present their reflections and arguments on paper. This is a life skill. Jack Wilde in his wonderful book *A Door Opens* (1993) describes how his fifth graders write about issues important to them such as class rules and playground equipment. The same premise is true for older writers.

Writing reflections about portfolio entries certainly is one of the most energetic ways to engage writers in explaining themselves. Since the documents in the portfolios are their own, only the writers know the depth of the rationale behind the selection. Often writing reflections open doors of thought and connections.

Writing commentaries, arguments, position pieces, and editorials calls for extended thinking. "Write from your feelings and emotions," I tell students, "but think as you write. Be alert to connections that come within your discovery draft or initial brainstorming. Argue with information, facts, and examples. Do not rely on your good looks, winsome voice, or chic clothes. Here, your words stand alone. Make them count."

Appeal to the reader's sense of logic with information. Be fully informed. Do not hesitate to draw conclusions or predict. When writing a commentary, students are the purveyors of knowledge. They are in charge. No teacher can say the student is wrong, only that arguments or commentaries aren't strong, logical, or developed enough.

Some ideas include using the 2–3–1 rule for emphasis. The placement of the writer's best words, phrases, sentences, and arguments is crucial. I use samples from previous students as needed. In 2–3–1 order, writers place their example or anecdote with the most power at the end of the piece, section, or paragraph. The second strongest section goes first, with supporting details in the middle sections.

Step in your readers' shoes and predict their reactions and complaints. Enthusiasm will strengthen any comment. Let us know you care, which makes readers more likely to understand your point of view. Good commentators take sides; conflict is an essential part of opinion papers. Consider using a quotation from a known source, a metaphor or simile, and names, dates, and places from history or literature. All can add to the clarity and authority of the piece.

Another type of commentary for students is evaluating a custom, ritual, idea, or myth: Why three meals a day? Why not walk under a ladder? Does lightning zigzag? The story behind superstitions, Thanksgiving meals, fads, and clothing lookalikes are all open to observations. Comparing and contrasting can be effective commentaries when students base them on their own opinions: Who is the better pitcher or singer? the best mall or mail-order catalog? Which book is an author's best? Is it better to go into business or to go to college? The more the student thinks and takes a stand the better.

Columns are written for a specific audience, such as people interested in and knowledgeable of music, computers, pets, science, word play, geography, or sports. A good column is the meat in any publication (e.g., Lance Morrow in *Time,* and Mary Macrory in syndication).

Columnists take pride in their angles, insights, and versatility. This is where they can go beyond the facts of the news to offer their viewpoints. Opinions are the rule of thumb, along with personal or local anecdotes. A beginning reporter notches her pencil each step along the way to getting a column.

When writing columns, students should find their topic in a hobby, interest, or field of knowledge. Recognize the audience, then write to that audience. Remind them that their audience probably has some background knowledge, so don't talk down to that audience. Use names and terms the audience will recognize. Personal narration, the personal *I,* short newspaper paragraphs, quotations from authorities, original humor, and nonoffending gossip are all fine tools.

Persuasive Writing

If students have opportunities to discuss their arguments and opinions orally, they already have a basis for written persuasion. After reading several pieces of good persuasive writing, students can formulate their definition of this genre. At some point we have to stop telling students everything. Students who write commentaries, reflections, position papers, and editorials will be better prepared for this nonnarrative form of writing. If their background is weak, then perhaps several smaller persuasive pieces may be needed for practice.

Why is the school's baseball team demoralized? Why don't school plays attract larger audiences? Why is cheating declining or increasing? School or local issues that students care deeply about come alive in words. Since persuasion is a difficult form of writing, calls for higher-level thinking and problem-solving skills, and doesn't rely on chronological order, not all students will immediately succeed. But I believe they all have the right to try to make others see their viewpoint.

Reviews

Book reviews are usually designed as a means of seeing if students read a book. They get routine and boring. Reviews of a movie, television show, restaurant, new store, album, piece of software, art exhibit, stage show, video game, surfboard, type of track shoes, or magazine might enliven the topic. To get students thinking about their area of expertise, refer to the first days' survey sheets or have them answer questions such as, What areas am I an expert in already? and What makes me an expert in that area?

A review written for the general public is not just a summary. It is an opinion, interpretation, and recommendation, written in a personal tone and supported by examples. Reviews try to answer questions. Is it successful at what it is trying to do? What did the reviewer think of it and why? What are the good and bad points and why?

A review may include a brief summary, evaluation and recommendation, documentation with examples, revealing details, descriptions, connections to other items in the same area, and quotations from or about the material.

Before students select something to review, give them some criteria. They should like the subject area and be an authority—at least for our classroom. Teach students how they can access more information. Again, students should have read within the genre before they begin composing reviews.

College Application Essays

Another essay "test" is writing the college application essay. Though there is plenty of time to write it, there is still pressure and panic. The essay is meant to reveal to strangers who the student is and how he thinks. There is no "grade," but the quality does influence whether or not the student is accepted by that college.

Different colleges want different types of essays. Some prefer a risk taking essay, while others want a more traditional piece of writing. I tell students to know their audience. Typical questions include:

Give a brief account of an experience that has influenced your opinions or attitudes.
Create a fable.
Comment on your academic achievements.
Write an essay on the topic of your choice.
Discuss the reasons you decided to apply to this college.
What person, event, or experience has been meaningful to you?
Select a character from a novel that reminds you of yourself.
Write an autobiography.

Students should remember that the college person reading their essay will probably read three hundred other essays the same day. Because readers usually divide the application into yes, no, and maybe piles, the beginning has to be strong enough to avoid the no pile.

Before writing the essay, students review their activities both in and outside of school. Which best represents the types of challenges they will meet in college? Which best indicate the ability to work through difficult situations, solve problems, and think creatively? Which experience represents the willingness to stay with a project over time and achieve a goal? These are the types of things colleges and universities look for. Remember that the essay reader will expect a stronger, more finished composition because the writer has had time to think, search, and review.

The students should follow the same writing processes that help them write for school. They must answer questions clearly and not superficially. How have you shown growth? What do you want to do with your life? Why do you want to go to college? What are you looking for in a college community? What do you want to have achieved five years from now? Rehearsing by talking out the essay with a friend, teacher, or guidance counselor may help. How does it sound? Will it work? Live with your essay for a while. Though this takes time, reflection is better than writing at the last minute. In fact, since college essays are on the students' minds, I think class time should be set aside to help them. Students can look up information, select quotes, and really style every word, phrase, and sentence. The draft should be trimmed down to about five hundred words (check the limit on the application). Tell students to read it aloud for tone, voice, and power. Read the first fifteen words. How are they? They should be important and catching so you want to read on. Read the instructions once more to make sure you understood and followed them. Unless directed otherwise, type or print the essays on a computer. Double-check spelling. A serious proofreader is invaluable. Then mail the application on time.

These essays are meant to show potential, to demonstrate how students will contribute to that school, to see how they fit a given campus, and to see how independent a student is. Another purpose is to see if students can take advantage of the essay as an opportunity to think a problem through, to consider ideas, and to see if they have gained from their experiences. Sanford Kreisberg (1995) recommends schools keep a collection of these essays for their students to use as learning tools. Teachers and guidance counselors could write comments on each sample for further help.

Readers of these essays encourage students to be honest, sincere, and original. At some highly competitive campuses, everyone who applies is the editor, captain, or president of something and has high grades and excellent recommendations. So be reflective. Show what you can bring to that campus.

Letter Writing

Writing letters is a useful life skill and can be an enchanting form of self-expression. Read letters from famous persons now available in books: C. S. Lewis, J. R. R. Tolkien, Mark Twain, Lewis Carroll, Beatrix Potter, Thomas Jefferson, and John and Abigail Adams. The artful and mysterious exchange between Sabine and Griffin in the Nick Bantock trilogy is also remarkable.

We can use letter writing as a positive reinforcement for good work. Writing a note of approval wins results. Too often the only time a student gets a piece of writing from a teacher, it is in the form of a reprimand. Show them the joy of correspondence—the magic in receiving a letter with good news. If students complain about certain school rules, tell them to put their thoughts down in a letter to school administrators.

One successful letter-writing unit focused on my students' attempts to publish a letter to the editors of *Newsweek*. For several Tuesdays, I borrowed a set of the magazines headed for a social studies class taught by a friend, Rick Samara. (I knew he didn't use the magazines until the end of the week and if he doesn't read this book, he still will not know I borrowed them.) That gave my class time to read the letters and focus on one or two main issues each week. The following week we would study the letters connected to articles we'd read and began to list the qualities of letters that did get published.

After several Tuesdays, students determined the published letters showed qualities of brevity, strength, and timeliness. We felt ready. The following week we reviewed the current issue; each of us selected one article we felt strongly about. We quickly peer edited and composed our letters. I had arranged for a business education class to type our letters and envelopes that day. By Wednesday morning, the letters had been typed and were ready to be signed and stamped. One student brought them down to the office in time for that day's mail. We knew we were brief and timely, and hoped we had written strong letters. Over the next week we discussed the reality of getting published and wondered how many letters *Newsweek* received each week. On the following Tuesday, no letters from our class had been published. But the next week, there we were (since we knew only one letter from Manchester would be accepted, we decided to all take ownership). When class convened, John Pappageorge looked at me and said, "We made it, didn't we?" I never could manage a poker face. "Yes!" he repeated. "We made it." I shook the rolled up magazine and smiled. They all wanted to know who had been published. Then John, normally a quiet student, spoke up again. "I know who it is. It's always Mary. She's the best writer so it has to be her. It's always her. Who else would it be? I know her letter got published."

I didn't know what to say, so I just smiled. John sat with his arms folded over his chest. "Well, Ms. Kearns, am I right?"

I handed him the magazine opened and pointed to the letter. John closed the magazine and returned it to me, saying nothing. It was like we had planned this routine. The whole class asked, "Who?"

"It's me," said John.

And it was. John Pappageorge, a junior at Memorial High School, was being read by more people than will ever read anything of mine (as Tom Newkirk pointed out). John had written a letter disagreeing with the proposed boycott of the Olympics, arguing politics had no place in sports. John held his head up and walked tall from then on, but we all did. After all, we knew someone who had been published in a national magazine.

Library Searches

Today, it isn't knowing everything that counts. What matters more is knowing where to find current information, and then judge and use that information. Students new to a school need to know where to get information, usually at the library. Now many school libraries are also media centers, holding more than just printed texts. CD-ROMs and the World Wide Web are two of the new resources. How does the library affect writing?

There is the library report, whose sole purpose is to learn to use a library, and there is the research paper, whose purposes are to ask questions and to discover worlds. These are two very different types of papers, so make sure of your intent. Pam Harvey, a media specialist, suggests that we need to rethink our whole approach to research as a result of new technology. Do students reared on computers really need note cards? Hasn't the meaning of research changed? Rather than upset English teachers, these advances should recharge and challenge us as we head into the new millennium.

Sports Articles

Sports offer numerous opportunities for students to practice their observational skills and turn their information into writing. Sports reporting requires some background, but everyone can report what they see. In the spring and fall especially, the fields and tracks are full of athletes learning their games. I like students to observe, take notes, and then write a sports article that combines narratives, observations, and summaries. More experienced writers can use this as a time to write feature articles, sidebars, interviews, or personality profiles—the list is endless. I submit the best sports reports to the school paper for possible publication.

Travel Pieces

Though our students may not travel to exotic places, writing travel pieces is a crucial exercise in observing details, using facts, and finding new angles. They can write about any place they go—a mall, lake, ski area. No place is ruled out as a possible subject. And travel pieces can make students look again at the familiar. For instance, what color dominates your city? In London it is black of the taxis and red of everything else. In Manchester the color is brick red of the old millyard and corporation-row houses. What about your city?

Travel pieces fall into two types. The straight what-there-is-to-see piece contains descriptions, is ordered chronologically or geographically, and is objective, informational, and quick to read. However, the armchair traveler wants a piece that captures the mood, tone, and secrets of the place. Closer to a personal narrative, this type of piece is filled with anecdotes, interesting people, and sites not on the tourist trail. The authors include their own reflections, but still the travel essay should add up to something we come to understand about the place, whether we actually travel there or not. Try reading Peter Mayle's books on Provence, Paul Theroux on England and China, and Charles Kuralt and William Least Heat Moon on America.

LANGUAGE

In the study of language, we need to ignite students' imagination and creativity through clarity exercises, word histories, and challenges to their acceptance of any printed word. Students who do not have a wide background in word awareness and language appreciation could start a log of interesting words seen in reading and heard in other classes. English is especially rich in art, music, physical education, home economics, and industrial arts classrooms. And these students probably need more practice in reading their words aloud. Read Robert MacNeil's *Wordstruck* (1989) and any of Richard Lederer's books (e.g., 1987) to develop your own stories from class explorations.

Play with words like *marinate*. What else can marinate besides meat? What about other cooking words such as *saute, puree,* and *glaze?* Does reading our draft aloud to a receptive listener help us *deglaze* it? Are strong nouns and vivid verbs the *bouquet garni* of writing? And aren't words that tingle the sweet vidallia onions of writing?

Introduce a new word daily: *stonewall, download, downsize, watergate,* and *jet lag*. Encourage students to avoid colorless, overused words and cliches and to try a variety of words, expressions, and comparisons. They shouldn't settle for *run* when we have *sprint, scamper, scurry, swoop, tear,* and *bolt*. They need to collect specific vocabularies for common nouns: *bowler* for *hat, sloop* for *ship,* and *DC-10* for *airplane*.

You might need to review specific and concrete verbs and strengthening verbs with a comparison: "The sea tossed him like seaweed."

I find it useful to study the sports pages. Sports writers cover the same basic sports, so they hustle for colorful yet precise verbs and nouns to capture the spirit of each game.

Grammar

"Spelling, punctuation, and capitalization are necessary parts of writing," wrote Peter Stillman in *Writing Your Way,* "but they don't *amount* to writing" (1995). As teachers we need to ask ourselves if the study of grammar aids writers. Does it improve writing? What is the relationship between knowing grammar terms and rules and then composing? What is the purpose of teenagers studying grammar?

Grammar terms have no hooks to words students already know, so textbook grammar becomes a lesson in rote memory. What a waste. Grammar requires higher-level thinking and should be taught in a concentrated unit on the significance of the structure of language. The better the students grasp abstract concepts, the better the students understand grammar. Constance Weaver (1979), for instance, has written important things about grammar, language, and how we study both. The more any writer understands the structure and variety of language, the better and more naturally that writer can manipulate language.

Before you go and open up those grammar handbooks, remember the editors are probably not grammarians and they certainly do not know your students.

FOR FURTHER READING

Ackerman, Diane. 1993. *Natural History of the Senses.* New York: Random House.

Atwell, Nancie. 1987. *In the Middle.* Portsmouth, NH: Boynton/Cook.

————. 1991. *Workshop 3: The Politics of Process.* Portsmouth, NH: Heinemann.

Avi. 1992. *True Confessions of Charlotte Doyle.* New York: Avon.

Barbieri, Maureen. 1995. *Sounds from the Heart: Learning to Listen to Girls.* Portsmouth, NH: Heinemann.

Berg, A. Scott. 1978. *Max Perkins: Editors of Genius.* New York: Simon & Schuster.

Bulla, Clyde Robert. 1988. *A Grain of Wheat.* New York: Godine.

Calkins, Lucy. 1986. *The Art of Teaching Writing.* Portsmouth, NH: Heinemann.

Calkins, Lucy, with Shelley Harwayne. 1990. *Living Between the Lines.* Portsmouth, NH: Heinemann.

Clark, William. 1990. "How to Completely Individualize a Writing Program." In *To Compose.* 2d ed., edited by Thomas Newkirk. Portsmouth, NH: Heinemann.

Cleary, Beverly. 1988. *Girl from Yamhill.* New York: Morrow Junior Books.

Cummings, Pat. 1992. *Talking with Artists.* New York: Macmillan.

Dahl, Roald. 1986. *Boy: Tales of Childhood.* New York: Puffin.

Dillard, Anne. 1987. *An American Childhood.* New York: Harper and Row.

Elbow, Peter. 1973. *Writing Without Teachers.* New York: Oxford University Press.

Fine, Anne. 1992. *The Book of the Banshee.* Boston: Little, Brown.

Fleischman, Paul. 1993. *Bull Run.* New York: Harper Collins.

Forman, James. 1992. *Becca's Story.* New York: Macmillan.

Fritz, Jean. 1982. *Homesick.* New York: Putnam.

Gallo, Don. 1992. *Author's Insights: Turning Teenagers into Readers and Writers.* Urbana, IL: National Council of Teachers of English.

Gallwey, Tim. 1976. *Inner Tennis: Playing the Game.* New York: Random House.

Greenfield, Eloise. 1993. *Childtimes.* New York: Harper.

Heat Moon, William Least. 1982. *Blue Highways.* Boston: Little, Brown.

Hesse, Karen. 1993. *Letters from Rifka.* New York: Puffin.

Hunter, Latoya. 1993. *Diary of My First Year in Junior High.* New York: Random.

Hyman, Trina Schart. 1989. *Self-Portrait.* New York: Harper Collins.

Kanin, Garson. 1971. *Tracy and Hepburn.* New York: Viking Press.

Kearns, Jane. 1996. "Time to Heal: One Student, One Paper, One Story." In *Meeting the Challenges,* edited by Maureen Barbieri and Carol Tateishi. Portsmouth, NH: Heinemann.

Kennedy, Ted. 1963. *New York Times.* November.

Kreisberg, Sanford. 1995. The Application Essay: Texts, Subtexts, and Teacher Intervention. *The Harvard University Letter* 11 (6): 4–6.

Lamott, Anne. 1994. *Bird by Bird: Some Instructions on Writing andLife.* New York: Anchor Doubleday.

Lasky, Kathryn. 1988. *Pageant.* New York: Dell.

Lederer, Richard. 1987. *Anguished English: An Anthology of Accidental Assaults upon Our Language.* Charleston, SC: Wyrick and Co.

Ledoux, Denis. *1993. Turning Memories into Memoirs: A Handbook for Writing Lifestories.* Lisbon Falls, ME: Soleil.

Lindberg, Gary. 1986. "Coming to Words: Writing as Process and the Teaching of Literature." In *Only Connect: Uniting Reading and Writing,* edited by Thomas Newkirk. Portsmouth, NH: Boynton/Cook.

Little, Jean. 1990. *Stars Come Out Within.* New York: Puffin.

————. 1991. *Little by Little.* New York: Puffin.

Lloyd, Pamela. 1989. *How Writers Write.* Portsmouth, NH: Heinemann.

Lyons, Mary. 1992. *Letters from a Slave Girl.* New York: Macmillan.

MacNeil, Robert. 1989. *Wordstruck: A Memoir.* New York: Viking Penguin.

Macrorie, Ken. 1984. *Searching Writing: A Contextbook.* Portsmouth, NH: Boynton/Cook.

Mayle, Peter. 1981. *Toujours Provence.* New York: Vintage.

————. 1989. *A Year in Provence.* New York: Vintage.

McPhee, John. 1969. *Levels of the Game.* New York: Farrar, Straus and Giroux.

————. 1971. *Encounters with the Archdruid.* New York: Farrar, Straus and Giroux.

Meltzer, Milton. 1991. *Starting from Home: A Writer's Beginnings.* New York: Puffin Books.

Mowat, Farley. 1993. *Born Naked.* New York: Houghton Mifflin.

Murray, Donald. 1978a. "Teach the Motivating Force of Revision." *English Journal.* October.

————. 1987b. "Write Before Writing." *College Composition and Communication.* December.

————. 1984. *Write to Learn.* New York: Holt, Rinehart, Winston.

————. 1985. *A Writer Teaches Writing.* 2d ed. Boston: Houghton Mifflin.

————. 1990a. *Shoptalk: Learning to Write with Writers.* Portsmouth, NH: Heinemann.

————. 1990b. "Teaching the Other Self: The Writer's First Reader." In *To Compose,* 2d ed., edited by Thomas Newkirk. Portsmouth, NH: Heinemann.

————. 1992. *Writing for Your Readers.* Old Saybrook, CT: Globe Pequot Press.

————. 1995a. "Why I Write the Personal Essay." In *Writing Lab Newsletter.* Durham, NH: University of New Hampshire Writing Lab.

————. 1995b. *Writing in the Newsroom.* St. Petersburg, FL: Poynter Institute for Media Studies.

Naylor, Phyllis Reynolds. 1987. *How I Came to Be a Writer.* New York: Macmillan.

Neumeyer, Peter. 1982. "The Creation of Charlotte's Web: From Drafts to Book." In *The Horn Book.* LVIII (5): 489ff.

Newkirk, Thomas, ed. 1989. *More Than Stories: The Range of Children's Writing.* Portsmouth, NH: Heinemann.

————. 1990. The Writing Process: Visions and Revisions. Introduction to *To Compose,* 2d ed., edited by Thomas Newkirk. Portsmouth, NH: Heinemann.

————. 1993. *Nuts and Bolts: A Practical Guide to Teaching College Composition.* Portsmouth, NH: Boynton/Cook.

————. 1994. *Workshop Five: The Writing Process Revisited.* Portsmouth, NH: Heinemann.

Newkirk, Thomas, and Jack Wilde. 1981. Writing Detective Stories. *Language Arts* 58:286–292.

Patterson, Freeman. 1979. *Photography and the Art of Seeing.* Toronto: Van Nostrand Reinhold.

Paulsen, Gary. 1991. *Woodsong.* New York: Puffin.

Romano, Tom. 1995. *Writing with Passion: Life Stories, Multiple Genres.* Portsmouth, NH: Boynton/Cook.

Rose, Mike. 1989. *Lives on the Boundary: The Struggle and Achievement of America's Underprepared.* New York: The Free Press.

Rule, Rebecca, and Susan Wheeler. 1993. *Creating the Story: Guides for Writers.* Portsmouth, NH: Heinemann.

Shaughnessy, Mina. 1977. *Errors and Expectations: A Guide for the Teacher of Basic Writing.* New York: Oxford University Press.

Soto, Gary. 1991. *Fire in My Hands: A Book of Poetry.* New York: Scholastic.

Stillman, Peter. 1995. *Writing Your Way.* Portsmouth, NH: Boynton/Cook.

Weaver, Constance. 1979. *Grammar for Teachers.* Urbana, IL: NCTE.

Welty, Eudora. 1991. *One Writer's Beginnings.* New York: Warner Books.

Wilde, Jack. 1993. *A Door Opens: Writing in the Fifth Grade.* Portsmouth, NH: Heinemann.

Zinsser, William. 1987. *Inventing the Truth: The Art and Craft of Memoir.* Boston: Houghton Mifflin.

————. 1990. *On Writing Well: An Informal Guide to Writing Nonfiction.* New York: Harper and Row.

————. 1991. *They Went: The Art and Craft of Travel Writing.* Boston: Houghton Mifflin.

6

Word Processing and the Writing Process Classroom

Word processors themselves teach us things about how pleasurable it can feel to be engaged in writing. . . . The computer has an enormous capacity to enhance the human potential for creativity, expression, and effectiveness in writing.
—Stephen Marcus, *Computers and the Teaching of Writing*

I was once told computers would take the place of teachers. The opposite happened: *we* are taking over computers, and computers have exploded in education with their power and possibilities. Our students are even more knowledgeable about computers as tools for learning, exploring, and wondering. We will be left in high-tech dust if we do not understand and utilize their potential.

MAKING THE BEST USE OF YOUR COMPUTERS

The One-Computer Classroom

Word processing on computers is a blessing for English classes, but having only one computer in the classroom forces us to make the best use of the computer every day. Avoid drill-and-kill programs. Use programs that enhance classwork! Drills on an expensive machine are no better than drills on purple ditto sheets. You may find teachers in your building using such programs, but before you jump in, ask yourself if using computers in this way teaches students better. Remember that our job is to teach students how to go about writing, communicating, and thinking clearly and critically.

How Can Computers Create Better Writers?

Word-processing programs can help our students be better writers by encouraging students to write before they compose—to brainstorm, plan, select, focus, draft, revise, and publish. And with an overhead monitor, you can project the computer's screen for the whole class for modeling work on the computer.

Computers can also force student writers to make choices and decisions about page setup, font and point size, graphics, and other style options. Computers assist careful rereading through printed drafts, which encourages students to make their own corrections.

Computers can also reduce writing apprehension. For some students, writing becomes easier to manipulate and motivation becomes higher. Connecting and integrating reading and writing are easier to establish with neat printouts. And computers also help students develop an understanding that errors can easily be corrected.

Writing activities in the one-computer classroom include drafting from notes or lists, brainstorming details, printing out a pencil-written draft, completing surveys and polls, writing letters, compiling a class book with a page for each student, using word-play programs, and generating word banks.

How Can I Make the Best Use of Time? Even if the computer is used every minute of class, each student will probably only get on the computer once a month. If you use this system the computer will end up being a high-class printer. Could students come in during lunch and study periods? Could groups of students work together on desktop publishing, design, and planning? Could partners work together over time to produce a project? Could students increase their computer time by using machines in the library? Should students sign up and use the computer only when they have something to edit? If you have a computer lab on campus, you could get all the students started with several days in the lab and then set up individuals on the single computer in your room.

Writing in the Computer Labs

Most schools already have one computer per room, and soon these will be networked to the library's multimedia resources. Eventually a student in your room will be able to tap into the Internet for research and communication. Even now you can walk into some rooms and see every student writing on a laptop. And computer writing labs are becoming reality, which will change our teaching. Writing in a computer lab will become more like the workshop environment of a newsroom.

For ease of use, I suggest that you show the students the computer lab rules and procedures before coming to lab. Let them know what their goals are, what they are doing, and how long they will be working in the lab so they can plan their time and work level. If you find yourself giving instructions or answering questions in the lab, keep the screens dark; once the screens turn on, users tend to turn full attention to them. Be sure to have clear procedures about when printing can and should be done. Print out computer directions and where to get help. Other suggestions:

Each student should have a disk, which should be provided by the schools; just like we hand out textbooks, we should be handing out disks for each student using the lab.

Have students print out draft copies and number them so there are several revision sections to show progress. As writing teachers we are concerned with revisions. If all the revisions, additions, and subtractions are done on the computer we will miss the work.

Talk about the spellchecker options. I have heard teachers say using a spellchecker is like cheating. Not true! Spellcheckers offer several selections and provide only correct spellings, unlike many insulting workbooks. Some spellcheckers show the word in context so there is rereading practice. Many also have word counts.

Discuss the use of a thesaurus—how, when, and why to use it. Selecting words is difficult, and not all the words listed have the same definition, texture, or tone. Because a computer thesaurus works in context, the lesson here can be stronger than in a regular paperback edition. As with paper writing, keep your grammar checker for later in the process.

Change is here. Some students, classrooms, and schools not only navigate the World Wide Web, they are writing their own homepages. Our school computers are making way for multimedia programs so students can produce documents filled with photos, movies, sound, and animation. The variety and depth of these authoring tools are limited only by our own imaginations. We are on the brink of a dynamite world of communication. It's a great time to be an English teacher.

FOR FURTHER READING

Marcus, Stephen. 1984. *Computers and the Teaching of Writing: A Resource Guide.* Cupertino, CA: Apple Computer Inc.

Thornburg, David. 1991. *Education, Technology, and Paradigms of Change for the Twenty-First Century.* Los Altos, CA: Starsong Publications. *What Work Requires of Schools: A SCANS Report for America 2000.* 1991. Washington, DC: Department of Labor.

Williams, Robin. 1990. *The Mac Is Not a Typewriter.* Berkeley: Peachpit Press.

7

Evaluating Without Grading

What is life or teaching without celebrations.
—Don Graves, *In Conversation*

Grading systems run our schools. Grades determine which classes and teachers students will have. They prioritize what matters and what doesn't matter. We even call the time blocks of our school year *marking periods.*

With this emphasis on grades, evaluation in the writing classroom evolved into a search for errors, a focus on what students cannot do or do not know. But the difference between grading and evaluation is enormous, as with asking if a glass is half empty or half full.

Grading is a relatively simple backward-looking drill. Evaluating is a complex and forward-looking action. Grading is a bureaucratic exercise that happens four or six times a year; evaluation is a learning, growing activity that occurs every day. Murray calls grading a "terminal response" (1985), where we rely on red pens to isolate mistakes.

If students think their writing will be searched only for errors, they just do the minimum. Students with this attitude feel no ownership, take no risks, and seek no discoveries.

GROWTH THROUGH GRADES

One former student, a fine writer, showed me a *C* on a way-below-her-ability paper, saying "It's not my grade; it's my teacher's. He made me do this topic I knew nothing about and am not interested in, so it's his paper and his grade." Each student "must develop the ability to evaluate his own accomplishment, to spot his own problems and to correct them" (Murray 1968).

In evaluation, the emphasis should be on the root word *value* and in the desire to improve student's writing and to note student's progress. In *Why We Hate Evaluating Writing: Legacies of Rousseau,* Andrea Luna (1993) argues that English teachers are at odds with our basic Romantic ideals in grading a paper: "We want to coach and judge it at the same time, a conflict of interest, like refereeing the same game our team is playing." Luna contends this leads to a "paradoxical view of evaluation that makes assessment problematic in a writing process classroom. . . . We cringe at giving a student a low grade on something she has worked hard and long on, because our students so often interpret grades on their work as grades on themselves."

Thankfully, I have never been bitten by this conflict of interest. I've always believed I could grade and I do. Though I prefer not to grade papers, grades are a fact of secondary education. But my students know that I do not see the grade as permanent. "Any paper can be improved. Any paper can be edited, revised, and submitted for another deadline," I tell them. My students also know they can discuss grades: "If the grade is too high, let me know and I will change it." I seldom have takers on this one. "If the grade is too low, gather your rationale and we'll talk." I have changed grades after listening to a student's impassioned defense. We make mistakes with grading; it isn't a big deal. A grade doesn't make a paper better or worse; it only makes it part of school policy.

My students select which papers in their folders they submit for evaluation. This puts the responsibility on their own lead pencils and reduces, for the most part, the interference of grades with student learning. I also let these struggling writers know that the grade today is solely an indication of how I read the paper yesterday. I know— and the students know—that another reading could illicit a different grade. I ask them if I missed something. Often I have students write me notes about their papers when they pass them in for evaluation to tell me what I need to know so I can be a better evaluator.

I follow three touchstones when evaluating students' writing:

1. To write well, students must be evaluated well.
2. Marking an error is not eliminating it.
3. Seeing an error marked is not understanding what is wrong or knowing how to correct the error for the next paper.

What can we do to note progress and problem areas in writing? For several years, I listed the name of each student in separate rows on one sheet with thirty-one columns. I would note attendance as well as what students were doing during each day's period. Each sheet logs a month.

Mary Ellen Giacobbe developed a conference page that includes notes about conference topics and minilessons taught. I have also seen other teachers use a single page in a three-ring notebook for each student in the class. But this overwhelmed me; I like the condensed version of one sheet per class. It seems more manageable and within my range.

Be sure to collect drafts, prewriting sheets, and finished and unfinished pieces in folders. Student progress can get lost in a sea of papers. Writing classrooms use folders to collect drafts, prewriting, sketches, lists, and rewrites where writing development can be seen as students collect their papers over a good length of time. These papers need to be dated so we can review progress, potentials, and possibilities. In these folders along with Can Do lists, students record their work and the genres they have attempted.

Have students self-evaluate. Students can review their own work to look for growth, changes, and improvements and then write an analysis that becomes part of their folder and is shared with you during evaluation conferences. Students can write responses to questions that focus on self-assessment of writing strengths.

One summer, as I traveled through Ireland with friends, our rented car stalled in the heart of inner-city Dublin. The four of us, all alert intelligent people and expert drivers, had no idea what the problem was. We opened the bonnet and looked inside. We looked like we knew something, but we didn't.

We cleaned, checked, and poked each movable part, got back in the car, and it started. But we didn't know why. We would have no idea what to do the next time the car stalled except to repeat our mystery litany.

The same scenario is true with error hunting in student papers. Marking up a paper does nothing except illustrate that we know the errors and that the student does not or is careless. By implication, a focus on mechanics suggests that this paper is the goal. But the purpose of this paper is to learn, so the student can move to other papers. This paper is only as important insomuch as it helps the student write better in the future.

To write well, students must be evaluated well. For each writing activity students work on, they need to be guided. They need feedback and reactions and questions *as they write.* Tom Carnicelli calls the error analysis of the completed paper an *autopsy:* the patient has died and now we try to tell you why.

WHAT ARE WE DOING WHEN WE GRADE OR EVALUATE A PAPER?

The emphasis should be on the word *progress,* which originally meant a royal journey with pomp and pageantry. Progress equals movement toward something better. I think it also implies the belief that students *can* improve. I like to keep that in mind when I am evaluating; it helps me look at students' writing with a more positive outlook.

One way to strive toward evaluating rather than just marking a paper is to read the paper entirely without a pen or pencil in hand. This is difficult for teachers. Instead, on a note you'll give to the student, first write the student's name. Without marking the paper, read the entire piece for interest, content, and clarity. To remember details, write notes to yourself on a separate pad of paper. Look for the overall impression. What is the person saying? How well was this goal accomplished? Review drafts and sketches to see changes and process. On the student's note, start with a line about your overall impression; you may even summarize what the person said to you (see Elbow 1973). Then identify the strongest part of the paper. What did you enjoy? What surprised you? We must find something to value (once I even praised margins). Otherwise, why should the student try on the next paper? Recommend one or two problem areas that the student could work on next time, one that the student can quickly remedy, and another longer and more involved correction.

Whenever possible, hold a conference with this student as you return the paper. Students may have questions or information that is not clear on the paper if read without context. Ask what they are working on now. What is the goal in this new paper? How will they achieve this goal? Where are they going to learn this or receive help? Do they have a plan? Leave them with the feeling that you like reading their papers and are interested in learning about the next topic and seeing how it develops. This type of reading and evaluating papers will not take as long as you think. Remember you know the paper quite well already since you have seen or heard it several times in class.

As we read and evaluate and grade papers, we need to keep in mind the different levels within the same class. Recognize those who can be nudged harder and sooner. Recognize and appreciate those who take more time to process. Writing is not an easy craft to master, but we can help by celebrating the individual. Recognize as well that mistakes aren't always failures. What may appear on first reading to be a mistake may on a closer look be an indication of risk taking.

Once we identify a problem, try to leave the student with options. There is never just one way to eliminate a mistake; the students will not have you around longer than a semester or two. When you identify a pattern of errors or composing problems, ask students why they make these mistakes. They may already know the answer and, if not, just thinking that the mistakes falls under one area and not several may help them be more confident within their own process. Writers need to carry their own writing first-aid kits.

Keep an inventory of little solutions to big problems—options and strategies to offer writers. Sometimes solutions are minute: the student needs a change of writing utensils or location or a break from sitting still. Other times the student needs a listener. How to recognize needs is part of understanding and appreciating the rhythms of the class and the working habits of each student. Put responsibility on students. "I noticed you misspelled many words in this paper. Why was that? What happened?"

Sometimes the student is just stuck physically or psychologically. All writers know that once in a while you need to defrost the refrigerator, clean the hall closet, or (my favorite) take a long drive. We can't provide these breaks in the classroom so I offer these possible solutions:

Here, try my pen. It's doing fine for me today.
Go sharpen your pencil.
Go get a drink of water and stretch your legs.
Would you help Sue? She's writing a paper like the one you wrote last
  month.
Try writing at my desk.
Ask Peter to write five or ten questions about details you need.
Go interview someone about that topic.
Put it at the back of the folder and work on something less aggravating.

When I first started teaching I did not do this. I graded and corrected as I had been corrected, thoroughly and with vigor. I slapped on grades. To this day some former students, call me "B+" Kearns. This was during my four-star general stage when I fought a war for perfection. I am embarrassed about that side of my teaching life and apologize to all those I affected. As I grew as a person and a teacher and started to write with my students, I learned to evaluate toward the future and not the past. From personal experience I learned what unknowing comments can do, how cruel and dead-ended grammar corrections can be, and how grades can close off thinking and discovering. When I read and review writing now, I look for signs of growth:

Will the student work on one piece over several days?
Is there evidence of prewriting, listing, brainstorming, revising, or rethinking?
Is the student attempting variety in forms and subjects?
Are there signs of growth in word choice, order, and details?
Does the student seem to understand writing as a process?
Is the student willing to ask for help when needed?
Is the student willing to help others when needed?

I recognize these signs of progress and celebrate their existence, encouraging students to understand their own writing base for future growth. I look for the ability to write standard American English, fluency through longer sentences, precise and developed word choice, a willingness to write, a sense of the value of writing and communicating, and the openness to peer edit, listen to other papers, and share the process of successful papers.

In the "final" grade on a paper, I now like to give separate but equal marks in five areas: content, form, process, surprise, and potential. Grading for a variety of elements allows me to do more teaching. I don't offer this method as the only approach; it is just something that works for me. Remember these grades should be considered as one small part of the daily evaluation going on in any writing process classroom. Writers do not fit a bell curve. A grade will not make an author, but the hunt for errors can destroy a writer. As Applebee and Langer (n.d.) state in *Assessment and Response to Student Writing,* "If evaluation is separated from instruction, if criteria for evaluation are kept consistent with those stressed during instruction, and if response becomes a responsibility shared with students as well as the teacher, assessment can become an effective complement to the process of learning to write."

HOW DO PORTFOLIOS HELP STUDENT WRITERS?

Traditional evaluation is always imposed from the outside, whether it comes from teachers or students. In the Manchester, New Hampshire, Literacy Portfolio Project, teachers, students, and researchers look at portfolios as a way to go beyond traditional testing and grading to develop the ability to self-evaluate. More than just school work is included in our portfolios. Learning goes on all the time, so students are encouraged to extend the contents of the portfolio to include outside-school items and make more connections with students at home, play, or work. With our comprehensive portfolios, validity is given to all informal learning after school hours.

For each item placed in our portfolios, we write a reflective explanation. Why is this item important? What does it show about us as a reader, writer, learner, and whole person? One student said, "I wish we had portfolios in math. I do fine on daily work, but I freeze in tests. In my portfolio I would leave out the tests. They don't show what I can do."

Through the collection and reflection process, students compile portfolios based on what they understand about themselves. Students explore their strengths and weaknesses, furnishing themselves and us with more of the history behind a piece of school work. Tests give teachers what *we* judge to be important at that moment, but through our portfolios we learn what students understand to be important.

I think the power of these portfolios rests in frequent evaluation, even on a daily basis. Classes are constantly considering what to place in them and why. The portfolio sample represents them individually as a reader, writer, and learner. We review our portfolios frequently, then add, delete, and again reflect.

Our reflections set the framework for students' ability to develop their goals and plans. "The key is their words about their reading and writing and about themselves as readers and writers," Jane Hansen (1994) says. "It is not only the content of the portfolio that is important, but the way the items get in the portfolios and what is done with the portfolios." These reflections help us go beyond our evaluations to see where a student worked hard on a problem or tried something new. We wouldn't have known the history without the reflections.

Students who have already been asked their opinions and have been shown that their opinions are valuable are more prepared to give honest comments, to share, and to respond to others. These reflections are a new writing genre, and students like teachers need time to practice and models to hone their ability to write reflectively.

Once we review our portfolios and look for patterns, we set goals for ourselves. The seventh-grade students of Joanne Coughlin went further by writing plans to accomplish their goals. They established their own lesson plans for the last month of school by these goals and plans.

Research teachers Diane Conway and Karen Harris asked questions as an ongoing theme in class: What can you already do? What do you need or want to learn next? What goals do you have? What plans do you have to accomplish these goals? What proof will you offer to demonstrate your goal?

Research director Jane Hansen put the questions this way: What do I do well? What's the most important thing I've learned to do? What do I want to learn to do next? How do I plan to work on this? What will I put in my portfolio to document my work toward this goal?

Whether our collection of drafts is called portfolios, folders, envelopes, or files, writers need to look behind to see where they are going. They need to ask themselves questions, set goals, and make plans. Evaluating, Jane Hansen always says, should also be a *planning* activity.

Celebrating the work of becoming writers isn't a sign of watering down assessment or an easy grade. Celebrations offer reasons to stop and enjoy the moment while recognizing that there is much work ahead. But knowing what we can accomplish strengthens our willpower to begin again. Eudora Welty said in a television interview that publishing a story did not help her write the next one, but a published story did give her the assurance that she could write. Our students need that same assurance.

FOR FURTHER READING

Applebee, Arthur, and Judith Langer. nd. *Assessment and Response to Student Writing.* New York: McDougal, Littell.

Elbow, Peter. 1973. *Writing Without Teachers.* New York: Oxford University Press.

Graves, Donald, and Bonnie Sunstein. 1992. *Portfolio Portraits.* Portsmouth, NH: Heinemann.

Hansen, Jane. 1993. *Researchers Reflect: Writings from the Manchester Portfolio Project, 1990–92.* Durham, NH: Writing Lab.

———. 1994. "Literacy Portfolios: Windows on Potential." In *Authentic Reading Assessment: Practices and Possibilities.* Newark, DE: International Reading Association.

Luna, Andrea. 1993. *Why We Hate Evaluating Writing: Legacies of Rousseau.* Durham, NH: Writing Lab.

Murray, Donald. 1968. *A Writer Teaches Writing: A Practical Method of Teaching Composition.* Boston: Houghton Mifflin.

———. 1985. *A Writer Teaches Writing.* 2d ed. Boston: Houghton Mifflin.

Rief, Linda, and Maureen Barbieri, eds. 1995. *All That Matters: What Is It We Value in School and Beyond.* Portsmouth, NH: Heinemann.

Epilogue: To Learn

Literate people have a passion for asking questions, both big and small, a hunger for learning new things and for making connections. In short they have a particular stance toward the universe: one of constant engagement and learning.
—Don Graves, Discover Your Own Literacy

I'd always wondered about the theory that there are no two identical snowflakes until a science teacher explained that no snowflakes encounter the same conditions during their development. Teachers, too, are combinations of all our experiences accumulated up to now. We are works-in-progress. We bring unique histories to our teaching. When we walk into a classroom we come with experiences filtered through knowledge and beliefs. I have been working on teaching and writing since I first ran into Don Murray in the early 1970s.

I read more now than I did when I first started teaching, not only research on teaching and writing but *good* books and magazines in every field. I read now more as a writer, whether it is Tony Hillerman's *Thief of Time,* Terry Tempest Williams' *Refuge,* or the *Dream Work* poems of Mary Oliver. Four books I must have on my deserted teaching island are Nancie Atwell's *In the Middle* (1987), Shelley Harwayne's *Lasting Impressions* (1992), Tom Newkirk's *More Than Stories* (1989), and Linda Rief's *Seeking Diversity: Language Arts with Adolescents* (1991).

Four books I must have when I get off that teaching island are: *Poems 1965–1975* by Seamus Heaney, Frederick Franck's *Art of Seeing,* MacWeeney and Conniff's *Irish Walls* and Annie Dillard's *Pilgrim at Tinker Creek.* But I also need Marty Asher's *57 Reasons Not to Have a Nuclear War,* Jane Austin's *Emma,* Sue Bender's *Plain and Simple,* and Philip Isaacson's *Round Buildings, Square Buildings, Buildings That Wiggle Like A Fish* and, of course, a blank book for writing and. . . .

As teachers we need to know and appreciate all around us, not for any cultural literacy or trivial pursuit but to stay fresh. To constantly learn, I read magazines outside my special field of interest—*Discover, Architectural Digest,* and *Surfing.* Reading in new fields helps us appreciate the beauty, art, and technology in things we don't do and helps us understand the children of the 1990s.

Search for new premises with a healthy intellectual skepticism for trends and an awareness for what's happening in our classrooms. We need to visit classrooms that aren't in our subject area or on our grade level, observing and selecting the best teaching techniques. We can learn from math, whole language, art, and music workshops. We need to be students again, to know how it is to learn and fail and struggle and not quite understand. Teachers were often students who found it easy to go through lessons, exercises, tests, and quizzes. We need to know how hard it is to learn.

Isn't it ironic that we teach freedom of choice but staff development training is often so rigid and far from the instructing turn of mind. We should explore areas still being examined. We can be part of the discovery and surprises of technology, learning styles, and literacy education. We are just beginning to focus on ways people become literate.

In our writing classes we establish support groups between ourselves and students, among peer readers, and within the entire class. Teachers need this too. I was about to quit teaching in October 1979 because of the isolation. I was on an emotional and educational high from the Exeter Writing Program, but when I returned to my school I was so alone.

By talking with teachers, we make sense of what we are doing and what we see. Now the World Wide Web invites us to chat around the world. Access the National Council of Teachers of English (NCTE) Web site at www.ncte.org or the National Education Association (NEA) at www.nea.org. Contact the Learning Network at www.att.com/education/learning network. And look for the new page from the International Reading Association (IRA). Email me at JKerns58@aol.com.

Make contacts with other writing teachers in the school. Ask the students about which teachers help them write. Be a friend to that teacher down the corridor who keeps asking what your students are doing. Join your professional groups and read professional articles. See if there is a local, state, or area chapter of NCTE, IRA, or a state English teachers' group. Cultivate the knowledge and passion of bookstore owners. These are all circles inviting us in.

As teachers, we need to be in a safe environment for our own learning. We should be teaching so we can influence each other, where the shelves in the teacher's room are filled with books to borrow. A safe environment for teachers should include buildings in which principals remove dreary educational books from the office shelves and replace them with real books, where librarians create reading centers for teachers, and where teachers want to talk about their teaching and learning and reading.

And we must see the student blooming right in front of us. Some of my best teachers have been my students, and I'm now learning from teachers who used to be my students. "One of the beauties of teaching," Herbert Kohl (1989) wrote, "is that there is no limit to one's growth as a teacher." I like to give myself this assignment: with a camera and thirty-six exposures, I see how far I can walk the beach before I take all of my shots. How long into the day can we go before we can see thirty-six new angles in our classes? Seeing gives us energy to nurture learning.

Learning means knowing that walking on the shore, photographing some old barns and apple trees, or listening to water run over rocks is as important as attending a lecture or serving on a curriculum committee. For every report we fill out or lesson plan we write, we should read a poem or, better yet, write a poem.

Learning gives us a sense of where we are going. And as these learning circles get larger and larger, the centers of energy cross and infuse one another. When my niece was a high school senior, she said, "Do you know what? There aren't any Cliff Notes for *Gone with the Wind*. I'm going to have to read the whole book." There aren't any Cliff Notes for teaching either.

It's a great and challenging time to be a teacher. So many angles of vision from so many classrooms are accessible to us now. I'm developing a sharper, stronger, livelier sense of where I am going. I'm going to be a teacher. You come too.

FOR FURTHER READING

Applebee, Arthur, and Judith Langer. n.d. *Assessment and Response to Student Writing*. New York: McDougal, Littell.

Atwell, Nancie. 1987. *In the Middle*. Portsmouth, NH: Boynton/Cook.

Braided Lives: An Anthology of Multicultural American Writing. 1991. St. Paul: Minnesota Humanities Commission.

Calkins, Lucy, with Shelley Harwayne. 1990. *Living Between the Lines*. Portsmouth, NH: Heinemann.

Delany, Sarah, and A. Elizabeth Delany, with Amy Hill Heath. 1993. *Having Our Say: The Delany Sisters' First One Hundred Years*. New York: Dell.

Elbow, Peter. 1973. *Writing Without Teachers*. New York: Oxford University Press.

———. 1981. *Writing with Power: Techniques for Mastering the Writing Process*. New York: Oxford University Press.

Fletcher, Ralph. 1992. *What a Writer Needs*. Portsmouth, NH: Heinemann.

Graves, Donald. 1983. *Writing: Teachers and Children at Work*. Portsmouth, NH: Heinemann.

———. 1990. *Discover Your Own Literacy*. Portsmouth, NH: Heinemann.

———. 1991. *Build a Literate Classroom*. Portsmouth, NH: Heinemann.

———. 1994. *A Fresh Look at Writing*. Portsmouth, NH: Heinemann.

Hansen, Jane. 1987. *When Writers Read*. Portsmouth, NH: Heinemann.

———. 1993. *Researchers Reflect: Writings from the Manchester Portfolio Project, 1990–92*. Durham, NH: Writing Lab.

———. 1994. "Literacy Portfolios: Windows on Potential." In *Authentic Reading Assessment: Practices and Possibilities*. Newark, DE: International Reading Association.

Harwayne, Shelley. 1994. *Lasting Impressions*. Portsmouth, NH: Heinemann.

Heard, Georgia. 1989. *For the Good of the Earth and Sun: Teaching Poetry*. Portsmouth, NH: Heinemann.

———. 1995. *Writing Toward Home: Tales and Lessons to Find Your Way*. Portsmouth, NH: Heinemann.

John-Steiner, Vera. 1985. *Notebooks of the Mind: Explorations of Thinking*. New York: Harper and Row.

Lamott, Anne. 1994. *Bird by Bird: Some Instructions on Writing and Life*. New York: Anchor Doubleday.

Langer, Judith A. 1992. "Rethinking Literature Instruction." In *Literature Instruction: A Focus on Student Response*, edited by Judith A. Langer. Urbana, IL: NCTE.

Macrorie, Ken. 1976. *Telling Writing*. Rochelle Park, NJ: Hayden.

———. 1984. *Searching Writing: A Contextbook*. Portsmouth, NH: Boynton/ Cook.

Murray, Donald. 1968. *A Writer Teaches Writing: A Practical Method of Teaching Composition*. Boston: Houghton Mifflin.

———. 1978a. "Write Before Writing." *College Composition and Communication* (December).

———. 1978b. "Teach the Motivating Force of Revision." *English Journal* (October).

———. 1984. *Write to Learn*. New York: Holt, Rinehart and Winston.

———. 1985. *A Writer Teaches Writing*. 2d ed. Boston: Houghton Mifflin.

———. 1990a. *Read to Write*. Fort Worth, TX: Holt, Rinehart and Winston.

———. 1990b. *Shoptalk: Learning to Write with Writers*. Portsmouth, NH: Heinemann.

———. 1990c. "Teaching the Other Self: The Writers's First Reader." In *To Compose*, 2d ed., edited by Thomas Newkirk. Portsmouth, NH: Heinemann.

———. 1992. *Writing for Your Readers*. Old Saybrook, CT: Globe Pequot Press.

———. 1995a. "Why I Write the Personal Essay." In *Writing Lab Newsletter*. Durham: University of New Hampshire Writing Lab.

———. 1995b. *Writing in the Newsroom*. Saint Petersburg, FL: Poynter Institute for Media Studies.

———. 1996. *Crafting a Life in Essay, Story, Poem*. Portsmouth, NH: Boynton/Cook.

Newkirk, Thomas. 1986. *Only Connect: Uniting Reading and Writing*. Portsmouth, NH: Boynton/Cook.

———. 1989. *More Than Stories: The Range of Children's Writing*. Portsmouth, NH: Heinemann.

Newkirk, Thomas, ed. 1994. *Workshop Five: The Writing Process Revisited*. Portsmouth, NH: Heinemann.

Patterson, Freeman. 1979. *Photography and the Art of Seeing*. Toronto: Van Nostrand Reinhold.

Postman, Neil, and Charles Weingartner. 1969. *Teaching as a Subversive Activity*. New York: Delta.

Probst, Robert E. 1988. *Response and Analysis: Teaching Literature in Junior and Senior High School*. Portsmouth, NH: Boynton/Cook.

Rief, Linda. 1991. *Seeking Diversity: Language Arts with Adolescents*. Portsmouth, NH: Heinemann.

———. 1994. "Threads of Life: Reading, Writing, and Music." In *Voices from the Middle* 1 (1):18–25.

Rief, Linda, and Maureen Barbieri, eds. 1994. *Workshop Six: The Teacher as Writer*. Portsmouth, NH: Heinemann.

———. 1995. *All That Matters: What Is It We Value in School and Beyond*. Portsmouth, NH: Heinemann.

Romano, Tom. 1987. *Clearing the Way: Working with Teenage Writers*. Portsmouth, NH: Heinemann.

———. 1995. *Writing with Passion: Life Stories, Multiple Genres*. Portsmouth, NH: Boynton/Cook.

Rose, Mike. 1989. *Lives on the Boundary: The Struggle and Achievement of America's Underprepared*. New York: The Free Press.

Rosenblatt, Louise. 1938. *Literature as Exploration*. New York: Appleton-Century.

Rule, Rebecca, and Susan Wheeler. 1993. *Creating the Story: Guides for Writers*. Portsmouth, NH: Heinemann.

Shaughnessy, Mina. 1977. *Errors and Expectations: A Guide for the Teacher of Basic Writing*. New York: Oxford University Press.

Smith, Frank. 1986. *Insult to Intelligence: The Bureaucratic Invasion of Our Classrooms*. Portsmouth, NH: Heinemann.

Welty, Eudora. 1984. *One Writer's Beginnings*. Cambridge, MA: Harvard University Press.

What Work Requires of Schools: A SCANS Report for America 2000. 1991. Washington, DC: Department of Labor.

Wheeler, Thomas C. 1980. *The Great American Writing Block: Causes and Cures of the New Illiteracy.* New York: Viking.

Wilde, Jack. 1993. *A Door Opens: Writing in the Fifth Grade.* Portsmouth, NH: Heinemann.

Young, Art, and Toby Fulwiler, eds. 1986. *Writing Across the Disciplines: Research into Practice.* Portsmouth, NH: Boynton/Cook.

Zinsser, William. 1988. *Writing to Learn.* New York: Harper and Row.

———. 1990. *On Writing Well: An Informal Guide to Writing Nonfiction.* New York: Harper and Row.

Appendix: Reading Lists

The days of students spending most of their time reading a single book in common, writing on a set theme topic, and reciting or discussing answers to teacher-centered questions are waning.

—Stephen Tchudi,
Planning and Assessing the Curriculum in English Language Arts

MY JUNIOR-HIGH LIBRARY SUGGESTIONS

In the best of worlds, teachers would be allowed to choose whatever books we would like to have on our classroom book shelf. Just in case you are asked (I never have been), here are some suggestions to get you started building your junior-high bookshelf.

A Brief Annotated Author List

Bill Brittain. Many students will be familiar with Brittain's *Wish Givers* (1986, Trophy), which fourth and fifth graders love. His *Fantastic Freshman* (1990, Trophy) is funny and realistic.

Jean Craighead George. Students know George from *Julie of the Wolves* (1974, HarperCollins) and the more recent *Julie* (1994, HarperCollins). Junior-high students should also read her *Shark Beneath the Reef* (1989, HarperCollins), about a Mexican youth trying to decide between shark hunting and marine biology; *The Talking Earth* (1987, HarperCollins), on the Seminoles and the Florida Everglades; and *Water Sky* (1987, HarperCollins), about Alaskan whaling camps.

Gordon Korman. He started writing for an English assignment when he was twelve and has continued his wry look at teens through *Don't Care High* (1986, Scholastic), *A Semester in a Life of a Garbage Bag* (1987, Scholastic), and *Losing Joe's Place* (1991, Scholastic).

Lois Lowry. *The Giver* (1993, Houghton Mifflin) is excellent, but if your students haven't read her *Number the Stars* (1990, Dell), start there, move to *Summer to Die* (1984, Bantam), and then *Find a Stranger, Say Goodbye* (1978, Houghton Mifflin). Read *The Giver* last.

Margaret Mahy. A superior writer and storyteller, Mahy charms us with her strong characterizations, dialogue, and New Zealand sense of wonder in *Memory* (1989, Dell), *Catalogue of the Universe* (1986, Macmillan), *Changeover* (1984, Macmillan), and *Tricksters* (1987, Macmillan). In *Catalogue of the Universe,* two strong women characters struggle to understand each other's problems. Mahy often blends stories with supernatural overtones. In *Memory,* a nineteen-year-old is driven by his memories while an eighty-year-old has lost his memory to Alzheimer's.

Walter Dean Myers. A three-time Newbury Award winner, Myers shows a variety of young African Americans growing up today in America. In his outstanding *Fallen Angels* (1989, Scholastic), he brings us into the world of a young soldier in the Vietnam War. *Fallen Angels* would work well with *Red Badge, April Morning,* and *Johnny Tremain. Hoops* (1981, Delacorte) and *Scorpions* (1988, HarperCollins) are two other excellent novels by Myers.

Gary Paulsen. Paulsen typically writes survival stories, usually about young boys on their own as in *Haymeadow* (1992, Doubleday). Keep a complete set of Paulsen as his books can be read and reread at any age. Paulsen is a writer with exciting and marvelous language. His books cover several reading levels, from easy in *The Island* (1990, Dell) and *Canyons* (1991, Dell) to sophisticated in *Winter Room, Winter Storm* (1989, Orchard Books) and *The Monument* (1991, Delacorte). *NightJohn* (1993, Doubleday) follows a twelve- year-old slave girl in the 1850s. Even if these books have been read in intermediate grades, students can reread them in junior or senior high for insights into American history.

Recent Classics

Linda Crew, *Children of the River* (1991, Dell). A novel of Asian refugees.

Michelle Magorian, *Good Night, Mr. Tom* (1982, HarperCollins). The relationships of an abused boy and his adult caretaker during World War II.

Carol Matas, *Daniel's Story* (1993, Scholastic). A fictional account of the Holocaust and a young boy's concentration camp experiences.

Cynthia Rylant, *Missing May* (1992, Orchard Books). Rylant won the Horn Book Award for this.

Graham Salisbury, *Blue Skin of the Sea* (1992, Doubleday). Through eleven short stories, we watch a Hawaiian boy trying to understand his family in the 1960s. The sea is a powerful character in its own right.

Gary Soto, *Baseball in April, A Summer Life* (1990, Harcourt Brace), and *Taking Sides* (1992, Harcourt Brace). All three titles concern growing up Mexican American in California.

Suzanne Fisher Staples, *Shabanu: Daughter of the Wind* (1991, Knopf). A young girl struggles for identity as a member of one of Pakistan's nomadic groups.

Budge Wilson, *The Leaving* (1993, Scholastic). This book of short stories won the Canadian Young Adult Book Award.

Nature and Animal Books

Jim Arnosky, *Gray Boy* (1988, Lothrup). A little treasure filled with awareness and observation—great for reluctant readers.

Avi. *True Confessions of Charlotte Doyle* (1992, Avon).

Farley Mowat, *Dog Who Wouldn't Be* (1981, Bantam), *Never Cry Wolf* (1983, Bantam), and *Whale for the Killing* (1984, Bantam).

Seymour Simon, *Galaxies* (1991, Morrow), *Icebergs and Glaciers* (1987, Morrow), and other Simon titles are presented in a picture-book style but are excellent for initial research.

Unique Narrations

Avi, *Nothing But the Truth* (1991, Orchard Books). A student uses a variety of methods to defend his rights.

Paul Fleischman, *Bull Run* (1993, HarperCollins). Through the viewpoint of sixteen different people, we relive the first Battle of Bull Run in 1861.

Karen Hesse, *Letters from Rifka* (1993, Puffin). A book set in Europe that brings the Holocaust closer to us through letters.

Mary Lyons, *Letters from a Slave Girl* (1992, Macmillan). A book with captivating insights into slavery and its horrors.

Paul Zindel, *A Begonia for Miss Applebaum* (1990, Bantam). Two teens—a boy and girl—narrate alternate chapters as they get to know their former science teacher, the retired and eccentric Miss Applebaum. There is humor and warmth with many potential discussion issues.

Fantasy

Jean Auel, *The Clan of the Cave Bear* (1994, Bantam).
Madeline L'Engle, *A Wrinkle in Time* (1976, Dell).
Paul Fleischman, *Graven Images* (1987, HarperCollins).

Fiction

Writers Mildred Taylor, Katherine Paterson, Robert Cormier, Christopher Collier, Jamake Highwater, Robin McKinley, Cynthia Voight, and William Sleator.

Informational

Beverly Cleary, *Girl from Yamhill* (1988, Morrow).
Lois Duncan, *Who Killed My Daughter?* (1992, Delacorte). A compelling real-life mystery.
David Feldman, *Why Clocks Run Clockwise and Other Imponderables* (1987, Harper & Row). Students love trivia.
Russell Freedman, Biographies of Eleanor Roosevelt (1993, Houghton Mifflin) and Abraham Lincoln (1993, Houghton Mifflin).
Jean Fritz, *China's Long March* (1988, Putnam) shows China as seen by an American author born overseas. *Homesick* (1982, Putnam) is also good reading.
M. Jean Greenlaw, *Ranch Dressing: The Story of Western Wear* (1993, Puffin). A fascinating look at jeans, hats, bolo ties, boots, and silver buckles.
Philip Isaacson, *Round Buildings, Square Buildings, and Buildings That Wiggle Like a Fish* (1993, Knopf). I would love this book to be given to me by a friend.
Roger Kahn, *The Boys of Summer* (1987, HarperCollins).
Brian Lanker, *I Dream a World* (1989, Stewart, Tabori, and Chang). A pictoral homage to black women.
Jean Little, *Little by Little* (1991, Puffin) and *'Til Stars Come Out Within* (1991, Viking).
Pamela Lloyd, *How Writers Write* (1989, Heinemann).
David Macaulay, *The Way Things Work* (1988, Houghton Mifflin). This title is filled with connections, offering students a way to read within an art-filled setting. Macaulay's research on cathedrals, castles, pyramids, mills, and what's underground are excellent study books.

Farley Mowat, Any of his books on nature are appropriate. Most concern the Canadian wilds, but *Woman of the Mist* (1988, Warner) is about Dian Fossey and *No Birds Sang* (1980, Warner) chronicles Mowat's war experiences. *Born Naked* (1993, Houghton Mifflin) includes his childhood writings in journals and poems.

Jim Murphy, *Long Road to Gettysburg* (1992, Houghton Mifflin). Firsthand accounts of this battle from the journals of a Confederate soldier and a Union soldier.

Christopher Nolan, *Under the Eye of the Clock* (1989, Delacorte). A writer tells his story of overcoming handicaps.

Rosa Parks, with Jim Haskins, *Rosa Parks* (1992, Dial). A woman in the center of the freedom fight.

Gary Paulsen, *Woodsong* (1991, Puffin). The popular author brings us with him to the source of his early books.

Sally Ride, *To Space and Back* (1989, Morrow). The story of her adventures within our space program

Other Book Lists

For further titles see the excellent lists in Linda Rief's *Seeking Diversity* (1992, Heinemann) on the themes of the Holocaust, prejudice, war, Native Americans, and generations. Nancie Atwell's *In the Middle* (1987, Boynton/Cook) has a list of student favorites. For a unit on peace and its possibilities, see Mary Rose O'Reilley's *The Peaceable Classroom* (1993, Boynton/Cook).

You can also get recent or specialized book lists from a variety of sources:

- The Children's Book Council. This group offers book lists and information about publishers. Contact the CBC Order Center, 350 Scotland Road, Orange, NJ 07050.
- *Children's Choices.* Single copies are free. Send a SASE to the International Reading Association, P.O. Box 8139, Newark, DE 19711. They also offer lists of books in the social studies and sciences.
- *Horn Book.* This periodical reviews new literature. The address is 31 Saint James Avenue, Boston, MA 02116–4167.
- Reviews in magazines. Browse in *Language Arts, Teachers Networking, New Advocate, Voices in the Middle,* and the *New York Times Book Review.*
- Friendly librarian at the school or city libraries and knowledgeable bookstore staff.

- Individual publishers. You might try writing them.
- The student. Always ask what they are reading.

MY SENIOR-HIGH LIBRARY SUGGESTIONS

Many senior-high readers are caught in an in-between stage: too old to be considered Young Adult readers and too young for more "serious" literature. Finding reliable reviews of literature for students between fifteen and eighteen is difficult. When in doubt, I go with books I like to read. As you get to know your readers, you can rely on your students' suggestions. I try to have a mixture of prose, poetry, fiction, informational, classics, and contemporaries. Students always enjoy books by Richard Lederer.There are many titles from the junior-high list I'd include—books by Mahy, L'Engle, Collier, David Macaulay, Myers, Paterson, Taylor, Voight, Soto, and Greene. You will see other overlaps as well.

Nature

Writers Annie Dillard, Lewis Thomas, Rachel Carson, Stephen J. Gould, Loren Eisley, Farley Mowat, Sue Hubble, John Muir, James Herriot, Henry Beston, and Sally Carrighar.

Mysteries

Writers Rick Boyer, Robert Parker, J. S. Borthwick, Jeremiah Healy, Linda Barnes, Barbara Neely, and Brendan DuBois take place in New England. Tony Hillerman and Walter Satterthwaith write about the Southwest. Sue Grafton prefers Santa Barbara, California. Martha Grimes sets her stories in English villages, as does Hazel Holt. M. C. Beaton writes of Scotland and the English Cotswolds. Ann Fallon, John Brady, and Bartholomew Gill set their mysteries in Ireland. Specific titles I'd suggest include the following.

Tom Clancy, *Hunt for Red October* (1985, Berkeley Press), *Patriot Games* (1987, Putnam), and *Clear and Present Danger* (1989, Putnam).
John Grisham, *A Time to Kill* (1992, Dell), *The Firm* (1991, Doubleday), *Pelican Brief* (1992, Doubleday), *The Chamber* (1994, Doubleday), and *The Client* (1993, Doubleday) are all good.

Classics

Jane Austin, *Pride and Prejudice* (1984, Bantam), *Emma* (1991, Knopf), and *Sense and Sensibility* (1983, Bantam).
Truman Capote, *A Christmas Memory* (1989, Knopf).
Walter Lord, *Night to Remember* (1983, Bantam).
Colleen McCullough, *Thornbirds* (1978, Avon).
Margaret Mitchell, *Gone with the Wind* (1976, Avon).
Boris Pasternak, *Doctor Zhivago* (1986, Ballantine).
Elie Weisel, *Night* (1982, Bantam).

Recent Novels

Douglas Adams, *The Hitchhiker's Guide to the Galaxy* (1991, Putnam).
Isabel Allende, *Eva Luna* (1988, Knopf).
Maeve Binchy, all titles.
S. E. Bridgers, *Home Before Dark* (1985, Bantam).
Olive Ann Burns, *Cold Sassy Tree* (1986, Dell).
Sandra Ciscernos, *House on Mango Street* (1991, Random).
Pat Conroy, *Water Is Wide* (1987, Bantam) and *The Lords of Discipline* (1986, Bantam).
Susan Cooper, *The Dark Is Rising* (1986, Macmillan).
Robert Cormier, *Fade* (1988, Delacorte).
Fannie Flagg, *Fried Green Tomatoes* (1987, Random).
E. J. Gaines, *The Autobiography of Miss Jane Pittman* (1982, Bantam).
Judith Guest, *Ordinary People* (1982, Viking Penguin).
James Herriot, all titles.
John Hershey, *Hiroshima* (1985, Vintage) and *Blues* (1987, Vintage).
Karen Hesse, *Letters from Rifka* (1992, Holt).
Jamaica Kincaid, *Annie John* (1985, Farrar, Strauss, & Giroux).
W. P. Kinsella, *Shoeless Joe* (1992, Ballantine).
Morgan Llywelyn, all titles.
Anne McCaffrey, *Dragonflight* (1986, Ballantine).
Robin McKinley, all titles.
Toni Morrison, *Beloved* (1988, Dutton), *Jazz* (1992, McKay), and *Song of Solomon* (1977, Knopf).
R. C. O'Brien, *Z for Zachariah* (1975, Macmillan).
Corrie Ten Boom, *The Hiding Place* (1984, Bantam).
Alice Walker, *The Color Purple* (1988, Putnam).

Informational Books

Diane Ackerman, *A Natural History of the Senses* (1990, Random).
Maya Angelou, *I Know Why the Caged Bird Sings* (1970, Random).
Arthur Ashe, *Days of Grace* (1993, Knopf).
Isaac Asimov, any title.
Sue Bender, *Plain and Simple* (1989, HarperCollins).
H. G. Bissinger, *Friday Night Lights: A Town, a Team, and a Dream* (1991, HarperCollins).
Claude Brown, *Manchild in a Promised Land* (1990, Macmillan).
Lorene Cary, *Black Ice* (1991, Knopf).
Sarah and Elizabeth Delany with Amy Hill Heath, *Having Our Say: The First One Hundred Years of the Delany Sisters* (1993, Dell).
B. Edwards, *Drawing on the Right Side of the Brain* (1989, Tarcher).
Nora Ephron, *Nora Ephron Collected* (1991, Avon).
James Fixx, *Complete Book of Running* (1977, Random).
R. Fulghum, *All I Need to Know I Learned in Kindergarten* (1993, Ivy Books).
Melissa Fay Greene, *Praying for Sheetrock* (1992, Fawcett).
Sue Hubbell, *A Book of Bees* (1988, Random), and *A Country Year* (1986, Random).
Garson Kanin, *Tracy and Hepburn* (1971, Bantam).
Garrison Keilor, *Lake Woebegone Days* (1986, Penguin).
Jean Little, *Stars Come Out Within* (1991, Viking) and *Little by Little* (1991, Puffin).
Peter Matthiessen, *Wildlife in America* (1994, Viking), and *Snow Leopard* (1987, Viking Penguin).
William Least Heat Moon, *Blue Highways* (1992, Little, Brown).
Tim O'Brien, *Things They Carried* (1991, Penguin).
Robert Pirsig, *Zen and the Art of Motorcycle Maintenance* (1975, Morrow).
Bailey White, *Mama Makes Up Her Mind* (1993, Addison-Wesley).
John Wideman, *Brothers and Keepers* (1992, Peter Smith).
Tobias Wolff, *A Boy's Life: A Memoir* (1990, HarperCollins).

Poetry

I recommend the poetry of Nikki Giovanni, Thylias Moss, Mekeel McBride, Maxine Kumin, Donald Hall, Ralph Fletcher, Mona Van Duyn, Marge Piercy, Mary Oliver, Seamus Heaney, Eavan Boland, Eamon Grennan, Robert Frost, William Butler Yeats, Emily Dickinson, Paul Janeczko, and Cynthia Rylant.

Assorted Connections and Themes in Picture Books

Monet
Christine Bjork and Lena Anderson *Linnea in Monet's Garden* (1987, R & S Books).
Richard Mühlberger, *What Makes a Monet a Monet?* (1993, Viking).
Mike Venezia, *Monet* (Chicago, Children's Press).

Authors
Joan Lowery Nixon, *If You Were A Writer* (1988, Macmillan).
Diane Stanley, *Charles Dickens: The Man Who Had Great Expectations* (1993, Morrow Junior Books) and *William Shakespeare: Bard of Avon* (1992, Morrow Junior Books).

African Americans
Donald Crews, *Shortcut* (1992, Greenwillow) and *Bigmama's* (1991, Greenwillow).
Peter Golenbock, *Teammates* (1990, Harcourt Brace).
Eloise Greenfield, *Night on Neighborhood Street* (1991, Dial).
Pat McKissack, *Mirandy and Brother Wind* (1988, Knopf Books), and *Flossie and the Fox* (1986, Dial).
Ann Turner, *Nettie's Trip South* (1987, Macmillan).

Dreams and Daydreams
Chris Raschka, *Charlie Parker Played Be Bop* (1992, Orchard Books).
Chris Van Allsburg, *Just a Dream* (1990, Houghton Mifflin), *Polar Express* (1985, Houghton Mifflin), and *Jumanji* (1981, Houghton Mifflin).
David Wiesner, *Free Fall* (1988, Lothrop).

Diverse Cultures
Jan Andrews, *Very Last First Time* (1986, Macmillan Children's Group).
Florence Heide, *Day of Ahmed's Secret* (1990, Lothrop).
Chris Raschka, *Yo! Yes* (1993, Orchard Book).
Allen Say, *Grandfather's Journey* (1993, Houghton Mifflin).
Ian Wallace, *Chin Chiang and Dragon Dance* (1993, Houghton Mifflin).

Ecology
Lynne Cherry, *River Ran Wild* (1992, Gulliver Green Books), and *Great Kapok Tree: Amazon Rainforest* (1990, Gulliver Green Books).
Gail Gibbons, *Recycle* (1992, Little, Brown).
Chris Van Allsburg, *Just a Dream* (1990, Houghton Mifflin).

Family Experiences
Eve Bunting, *Wednesday Surprise* (1989, Clarion).
Barbara Lucas, *Snowed In* (1993, Macmillan).
Bill Martin and John Archambault, *Barn Dance!* (1986, Holt).
C. Pomerantz, *Chalk Doll* (1993, HarperCollins).
Jane Yolen, *Owl Moon* (1987, Philomel).

Jealousy
Margaret Shannon, *Elvira* (1993, Ticknor & Fields).

Human Perfection
Tony Ross, *Super Dooper Jezebel* (1988, Farrar Straus Giroux).

Human Imperfections
M. Hoffman, *Amazing Grace* (1991, Dial).
Mavis Jukes, *Like Jake and Me* (1984, Knopf).
Bill Martin and John Archambault, *White Dynamite and Curley Kidd* (1989, Holt & Co).

Native Americans
Byrd Baylor, *I'm in Charge of Celebrations* (1986, Scribners), *Hawk, I Am Your Brother* (1976, Macmillan), and *Desert Is Theirs* (1975, Macmillan).
Tomie de Paola, *The Legend of Indian Paintbrush* (1991, Putnam), and *The Legend of Bluebonnet* (1993, Putnam).
Bill Martin and John Archambault, *Knots on Counting Rope* (1987, Henry Holt & Co).

Place Pictures
Byrd Baylor, *Best Town in the World* (1982, Macmillan).
Cynthia Rylant, *Appalachia: Voices of Sleeping Birds* (1991, Harcourt Brace).
Diane Siebert, *Heartland* (1989, Thomas Y. Crowell).

Truth
Margaret Mahy, *Great White Man-Eating Shark* (1990, Dial Books).
Jon Scieszka, *True Tale of Three Little Pigs* (1989, Viking Kestrel).

Summer
Marsha Wilson Chall, *Up North at the Cabin* (1992, Lothrup, Lee & Shepard Books).
Robert McCloskey, *One Morning in Maine* (1976, Puffin).
Gloria Rand, *Salty Dog* (1991, Henry Holt).
Natalie Kinsey Warnock, *The Wild Horses of Sweetbriar* (1990, Cobblehill Books).

Survival
Jean Craighead George, *Dear Rebecca, Winter Is Here* (1993, HarperCollins).
Barbara Lucas, *Snowed In* (1993, Macmillan).

Whales
Tony Johnston, *Whale Song* (1992, Putnam).
Melissa Kim, *The Blue Whale* (1993, Ideals).
Bruce McMillan, *Going on a Whale Watch* (1992, Scholastic).
Seymour Simon, *Whales* (1992, HarperCollins).